Promises

Promises

Based on a true experience with schizophrenia

ADAM JACK PELLEY

iUniverse, Inc.
New York Bloomington

Promises
Based on a true experience with schizophrenia

iUniverse books may be ordered through booksellers or by contacting:

iUniverse
1663 Liberty Drive
Bloomington, IN 47403
www.iuniverse.com
1-800-Authors (1-800-288-4677)

Because of the dynamic nature of the Internet, any Web addresses or links contained in this book may have changed since publication and may no longer be valid. The views expressed in this work are solely those of the author and do not necessarily reflect the views of the publisher, and the publisher hereby disclaims any responsibility for them.

ISBN: 978-1-4502-3162-6 (sc)
ISBN: 978-1-4502-3163-3 (dj)
ISBN: 978-1-4502-3164-0 (ebk)

Printed in the United States of America

iUniverse rev. date: 09/15/2010

DEDICATION

To my dad, Albert Jack Pelley.
Until I meet you again, "long may your big jib draw."

ACKNOWLEDGMENTS

To everyone who has helped me on this difficult journey of life and writing this book. My family, the doctors I have had in my life, to all who have been a part of this story. To everyone at Metro Community Housing Association, thank you for your care. To everyone at Novartis and the Mental Health Foundation of Nova Scotia, thank you for your guidance. To all the people at All Nations Christian Reformed Church in Halifax, Nova Scotia. Pastor Dave Vroege and Pastor Brad Close, thank you for your support. Thanks to Len Diepeveen for comfort and help. And to Harmony Kook, thanks for being a good friend.

A NOTE TO THE READER

This book is based on my life and my struggle with schizophrenia. I have battled mental illness for over ten years. Now I have molded my experience and journey into a story that I hope will take the stigma off of mental illness and show that people living with mental illness are unique and special.

Even though the Whynots may not be real, I hope you take the meaning of the story and know that everything I have experienced is as real as this book in your hand. Although doctors, family and friends have told me that my life is different than the reality that they know, I ask you only to do one thing: believe.

Some names have been changed due to privacy reasons; others have been used with permission.

Life
Poetry
Birth
Learning
Reminiscing
Death
Poetry

Table of Contents

INTRODUCTION

I'd made another trip home from the Abbie J. Lane Memorial Building psychiatric facility in Halifax, Nova Scotia, but my paranoia persisted. I wanted to watch television but I couldn't; my thoughts seemed to be broadcast through the screen. I stayed downstairs in my room. I couldn't spend time with family because I believed my thoughts were going through them. This sickness, this new reality, turned me into something that I could not recognize in my bathroom mirror. My reflection was not of the boy whose love of basketball would carry his day but of a man tormented by darkness, the world gripping him by the throat.

I was inside of the television, and in turn that television was inside of me. People on TV shows commented on the terrible thoughts that crossed my mind; there were good thoughts too, but they didn't care. Gossip is a burden not understood by love.

I was confused. Everyone told me that the world I perceived was not true, not concrete, that it was a world only real to my being, only true to me. Would anyone tell me the truth?

After good meals and listening to voices I couldn't see, Mom, my stepdad Ray, and I left the south shore of Nova Scotia and headed back to Halifax, making the trip in good time. A comfortable ride in Ray's red Buick. I looked at Mom. I could tell from her look, posture, and mood that she was very concerned. How long would I be in hospital? Would I ever find medication that worked? Where was her little boy?

"Adam, try your best to get some rest, and have a good talk with your doctor," Mom said.

"Okay. I love you, Mom," I said.

"I love you too."

The elevator took me to the seventh floor of the psychiatric facility. I pushed the button to the locked door and was let inside. There I saw a new patient, one who was agitated and restless.

"Can you hear what I'm thinking?" I asked, the same question I asked any new patient roaming the halls of the seventh floor.

"Yes, I can! I'm not lying anymore!"

Finally, it felt like someone was being honest. My reality was the same as everyone else's. One man struggling with illness brought truth to mine. I smiled and glanced at him for more answers. I looked at the nurse at the nurse's station, who was shaking her head no, denying what this new man had just told me.

"No one can hear your thoughts, Adam," she said.

Was this real? Was a man with manic tendencies telling me the truth for the first time, or was an educated nurse with experience in the field denying my reality once again? The new patient left the nurse's station, frenzied and talking to anyone even if no one would listen.

I went to bed, wondering about the new patient, wondering about the label of mental illness they gave me: schizophrenia. I just wanted the truth, whatever it might be. If what I was experiencing was real, voices were leaving me distanced from society, my thoughts were bringing me close to insanity. I still believed that one thing was certain: what was true to me, in essence, could be true to the world.

1. PROMISE

Love is the mystery that builds the universe. Turner wakes weary, trying to remember his dream, but it leaves him like a breath on a cold Nova Scotia morning. Trying to make out the numbers on the alarm clock, he wants to hit the snooze button but realizes he cannot. He has to see his patients, and he has to prescribe medications. As he rolls out of bed, his wife, Sherri, sits up, rubs her eyes, and begins to speak words that at this time of day can be interpreted only by her love, Turner.

"Good morning to you too, dear," Turner grumbles, rubbing his eyes, smiling at his spouse for the first time of the day.

Turner Whynot retreats to his bathroom and performs the early day rituals of the new millennium man: showering, shaving, brushing of teeth, flossing, combing of hair. Cleanliness is the carriage of couth.

As Turner wipes away the steam from his silver-trimmed mirror, he looks at his reflection and ponders his thirty-two-year existence: his life with Sherri; his short tenure as a psychiatrist at the Abbie Lane Psychiatric Facility in Halifax, Nova Scotia; his gradually receding hairline; and a pimple that has just broken out on the tip of his nose.

"Hurry up, I have to get in there," Sherri yells.

"Be one sec," Turner shouts back, stretching his slim, six-foot frame.

Sherri forces her way into the bathroom, strips off the towel that is around her husband's waist, and with all her strength pushes him out of the door, knocking him into the bedside table. She must get to work herself.

"Thank you, my dear," she smiles.

Turner laughs, picking up a picture that was knocked over. It is a photograph of his family—his sisters, his mother, and his father, the man he looked up to and respected. He remembers the one thing that always circled his conscience, the way the earth circles the sun: *the promise.*

Looking out the window, he sees that the day is damp and gray; there is a slight fog on the cove where they live, a wet reflection on the road that leads to the city about ten minutes away. Herring Cove is a collective calm, a contradiction to its neighbor, Halifax, the busy, boisterous, bubbling boomtown that sleeps only a couple hours a week.

Turner decides on the good suit. A black blazer and trousers, white shirt, canary yellow tie, and a pair of black shoes that are so shiny they will hurt your eyes if you look at them too long.

"Gotta go, Sherri," he shouts.

"All right," she replies. She's also running late and needs to rush to her bank manager job downtown.

There's no time for breakfast. He'll drink coffee only out of necessity, the local Tim Hortons coffee shop inviting him in for a cheap drink. Turner walks out of his home to see a seagull land on the top of his sleek station wagon. He looks at the bird and smiles and, to his surprise, the gull seems to tilt its head and smile back.

Turner laughs to himself and wonders how the diversity of nature complements the evolution of society. No sooner does his imagination overtake his thoughts than the gull winks at the doctor, turns around, sticks its ass in the air, and shits right in the middle of the car window. The seagull looks at him one more time and flies away, squawking as if laughing.

Turner doesn't know whether to chuckle or to think the bird insulted him the only way the bird could. Get mad or shrug his shoulders; smile or swear. Whenever or wherever confused, only one thing can clear his mind and allow him to proceed with his daily activities: *the promise.*

The promise defines who he is, what he does, how he conceives thoughts. The promise is why he helps the sick. The promise is why the sick talk to him. The promise is his being, yet the promise has never been completely fulfilled. Soon, it shall be.

Lacking the time to clean the shit off the window, Turner takes the old Purcell's Cove Road into Halifax. It is a picturesque trail, lined with mansions and boats whose owners wait to set their sails on the summer sea. A line of automobiles welcomes him to the restless Armdale Roundabout; his patience persists until he turns on to the quickness of Quinpool. The only stop before he reaches his office at the hospital is at Tim Hortons for coffee.

Files upon files are stacked upon his desk, from old patient discharge papers to a couple of *Sports Illustrated* magazines. A mess. But when Turner has to find something, he can sense that needle in the haystack. Usually, there are many clients to see, but according to the appointment book there are only two today and not at his office in the psychiatric facility. Once a week he travels down town to a place frequented by people who have a difficult experience with mental health."1221 Barrington Street, please," Turner yawns to the cab driver; he does not want to brave the traffic or struggle to find a parking space in downtown Halifax at this time of day. He notices a cross and rosary hanging from the taxi's rearview mirror.

Connections Clubhouse is the cornerstone at the end of one of the busiest streets in eastern Canada. Turner loves the clubhouse, the members, the staff, and the atmosphere. All in all, it is just a great place to relax and become reinvigorated. It is a place where Turner sees sick people get better; in turn, those people help others.

"Hello, Dr. Whynot," Trina says. "Laura is upstairs waiting for you."

Trina, the secretary at the clubhouse's front desk, always puts a grin on his face. Turner knows that she's never missed a day of work.

The yellow walls of Connections reflect its mission: to show that people with mental illness have ability and capability. The yellow walls make you want to walk these halls and, like the staff of the clubhouse, reassure the members that they are safe.

"Dr. Whynot, Dr. Whynot," calls a voice as the doctor makes his way to the second floor.

At the bottom of the stairs is a thirty-four-year-old woman, beautiful and beaming, very clean and proper, with more lift to her chin than any other patient that Turner sees here.

"Dr. Whynot, I need to see you today. It is very important," she says.

"Do not worry, Susan, I will see you today. But I believe I have to see someone else first, okay?"

"Thank you, sir." Susan's white teeth sparkle as if glaciers are growing through her gums.

Laura Lewis is sitting at her computer, typing a report; bipolar disorder has affected one of her patients to such an extent, Laura is recommending readmission. Although the patient has been hospitalized before, therapy and new medication may help in treatment and recovery. Laura is the on-site nurse at Connections. She attends to all medical needs and assists Dr. Whynot during his psychiatric sessions, coordinating appointment times, refilling prescriptions, and recording all things relevant between doctor and patient. Laura is reliable. Laura loves her work.

"You busy?" Turner asks as he knocks on the door.

"Actually, I am ready whenever you are," Laura says, picking up files and following Turner toward the boardroom where all meetings between doctor and patient take place.

Turner often wonders what it is like to be "mentally ill," what it is like to be the patients he medicates and treats so they can fully participate and be healthy in an active society. Sometimes he feels like a failure in his work—when the sick do not listen, and they're in and out of hospital like a man stuck in a revolving door, minds turning without rest. Satisfaction comes when people start to be active in civilization, when they are working, laughing, living. Their eyes become clear, and they understand the same reality that the rest of the world is functioning in, although the memory of their disability remains, whatever colorful portrait it becomes. Turner reasons that this is the reason university books are bought and studied.

They sit down in their chairs, and Turner hears a rap at the entrance, introducing someone who is confused about self and spirituality.

"Hello, Mark," he says to welcome the man, who is shaking, eyes bloodshot from lack of sleep and crying. Dressed all in black, he has teeth that almost match his attire, stained by coffee and years of smoking cigarettes. Still, he is clean shaven, with hair combed, and looks much better than the last time the doctor saw him.

"Doctor, I can't take it," Mark Daltry says, sitting in his seat.

"What can't you take?"

"Everything, the whole world is closing in on me. There is too much pressure." Mark puts his hands on his head to close his eyes, escaping for a second.

"And why all the pressure, Mark?"

"It's been like this for years. Only one thing could be doing this to me, putting all this weight on my head."

"And what is that one thing, Mark?"

"God," Mark states, looking up at the doctor and the nurse.

During the two years of Turner's relationship with Mark, the focus of therapy has been religion. Mark believes God is at the center of his problem. God determines every pain, ache, dilemma, and hallucination that affects the poor man's spirit. It has been like this since their first meeting. Prescription drugs, and therapy have toned down some of the symptoms, but Mark's belief that God is torturing his existence cannot be removed from his mind.

"Doctor, I get up every morning, and I know that the Lord is on my back," he says. "With everything that has happened in my life, I must keep going, with or without God. There is no answer in dying. It's hard being alone, but alone I am"

Turner and Mark had talked about suicide before, but the doctor is confident that Mark can function outside of hospital.

"Mark, how are the voices inside of your head?" he asks.

"Some are around, some are gone, but they are improving. But my real problem is with God." Mark blames all his hallucinations on a divine entity, a being beyond our senses. For Mark, few voices bring comfort; most cause chaos. The audible hallucinations are confronted directly by paranoia; the voices are more real than anything that is concrete. Mark sometimes finds quiet with medication. Turner, however, knows he doesn't take his pills daily.

"Are you taking your pills every day, Mark?"

"Yes," Mark answers with a broken tone, looking out the window and trying to change the subject.

"You know, if you took your meds every day the voices would go away."

"The voices will never go away for me because God never goes away."

Mark stands up to leave the room, fired up and feverish, digging into his breast pocket for his cigarettes.

"Hold on, you need your prescription refill." Turner writes out a prescription for olanzapine, an antipsychotic medication, 150 milligrams per day. "Please take this, and we will see you in a couple of weeks."

Mark had been diagnosed with schizophrenia before they met. Schizophrenia is the only label that has ever been put on his illness. Schizophrenia made Mark lose who he is, and it made him lose who he is in society. Schizophrenia is a thief of reality. Mark doesn't know what is real.

"Hello, Dr. Whynot," Susan Swim sings as she walks into the boardroom.

"Hello, Susan. Nice to see you. How are you?"

"I am doing very well," Susan says with a smirk.

Since the day that Turner first met Susan, she has benefited from therapy, always takes her medication, and realizes that she is suffering from a mental illness.

"I feel excellent," she continues. "I feel like I am getting better every day."

Turner feels his work is justified when his patients are feeling better and looking well. Seeing a patient advance, having a vision through the mist of illusion called "mental illness," his face filled with the light of hope and understanding makes Turner Whynot realize the reason he wants to help the sick recover from shattered thought and scattered ideas of silent mind. He thinks about his father looking successful in a two-piece suit and recalls the one thing that makes him who he is: *the promise.*

Turner can see recovery in Susan's face, a bounce in her step, and confidence in her stride. Although Susan has shown much improvement, the days of pacing hospital wards and the inescapable voices will always linger.

"Even though I am feeling much better, I can't shake that damn devil," Susan says.

"Why is that, Susan?"

"Because he always follows me, chases me. He will not leave me alone." Susan wants to cry, but fights the tears, clenching her fists, knowing what the doctor is about to say.

"Susan, we have talked about this many times. There is nothing following you; it is your illness that makes you think that there is some devil after you all the time. You have come a long way since the first time we have met. You understand what is going on around you and inside of you. That is the key for you to move on."

"I understand," she says. "By listening to doctors and to you, I am living now. I haven't felt like I have lived in about fifteen years. I know it's an illness. I accept that. But that idea that the devil will always be around is with me, I accept that too. It's hard to accept, but I accept it. This may be one of the biggest obstacles of my life, but I intend to overcome every obstacle I face. I live today for today, and I'll try to make sure that not even that damn devil can get me."

Susan stands up and extends her hand to shake Turner's. They both smile as if each has done his or her job to the fullest. Susan knows she doesn't need a prescription refill; she has enough medication at home. Her antipsychotic drug, clozapine, has turned into her nicotine. Her pills are her escape from the stress of schizophrenia, like smokers gaining release from stress with a puff.

"I am a little worried about Mark," Laura mutters as Susan closes the door behind her. "It seems as if there is no progression forward. Maybe the hospital is the best thing." A little flutter in her eyelids makes it look more like a plea than a proposition.

"With time, Mark will realize that all his symptoms, that his reality is unreal, that there are no spirits or God doing this to Mark," Turner replies. "I have studied this for years, and in my therapies and research I have come to one conclusion: there is no God or Satan doing these horrible or fantastic things to patients. It is all chemical imbalances and crossed neurons. When people listen, they get better. When they do not listen, they suffer."

Laura looks confused. She can't tell if Turner Whynot is an atheist or an adorer of every human soul. Either way, she knows he wants what's best for his patients. "I will see everything is recorded and documented," Laura says. As she leaves the boardroom, she looks over her shoulder and sees Dr. Whynot put his head in his hands.

Turner Whynot is not a spiritual man. Growing up, he believed in the message and teachings of Jesus Christ. As he got older, education, employment, and athletics became more important. After he became a doctor and started treating patients, the science of psychology became more important than the divinity of being. He believes five pills and a glass of water is better treatment than a Bible and a preacher. It's not that Turner doesn't believe in God; it just seems that God is not around when people need him.

Again, Turner remembers his father, and then thinks about himself, the man he has grown into, the man he has become. He remembers the promise.

With another coffee in mind, Turner decides to get lunch downstairs at the cafeteria. There, a meal only costs one dollar. The food is good. It fills that itch in your tummy, with more food on the plate than any fine restaurant in the city.

Turner does not see every member at the clubhouse. Out of the three hundred members, he sees about forty. Watching some of the members, it seems as if there is nothing inside of them, only an instruction manual, a remote control with broken buttons in their brain to eat, sleep and walk forward. Others are so full of life you would not expect a label of mental illness to be attached to them.

Walking into the lunchroom, he sees it is pretty full; there are not many seats at which he can enjoy his plate of BBQ chicken, roast potatoes, and mixed vegetables. As Turner lines up to get his food at the serving counter, he sees Mark and Susan sitting together, eating, nodding, and sharing a conversation. They don't seem interested in their meal, only in each other. The couple's conversation seems to pass off to others in the room, who also talk about their experiences. Throughout the room, people talk about how they deal with reality and the way society looks upon their stigmas, in all aspects of their lives. The Connections Clubhouse cafeteria is its own congregation, focused on food and the education of the broken conscience.

Turner is amazed at the way the people of the clubhouse seem to be one, like a tree that has grown to harvest the miracle of life. It makes him think that maybe goodwill and a healing energy inside that could overcome the illness that affects all in the clubhouse. But books and lectures have taught him that only crossed neurons and chemical imbalances can create a state of total mental disorder. Tomorrow, all things will come clear.

After finishing his last piece of chicken, Turner heads back up to the boardroom, packs his things in his leather briefcase, and says goodbye to Laura, while she records the last bit of notes from the day's meetings.

"Bye, Dr. Whynot," Trina says, as Turner runs out of the door. He neglects to say goodbye to the sweet secretary because of the hectic day and his thoughts of tomorrow.

He takes a taxi back to Abbie Lane but doesn't go to his office. Instead, he heads directly to his car, his focus now on home and the love of his heart. Tim Hortons is always on his mind. He stops for another coffee. He arrives home to find Spot, his huge, black Newfoundland dog, waiting for him; Spot had been sleeping when Turner started his day. Spot jumps up and tackles Turner to the floor; there is a smile on both their faces. Comfort can be found with all living beings; good intentions created a strong bond between Turner and Spot.

Turner changes his clothes, putting on his black-and-white Adidas tracksuit. He puts a leash on Spot and heads out to walk around Herring Cove. With the damp haze off of the water, the air is sweet, clearing Turner's lungs and making Spot's moist tongue hang. They walk enough to generate a small sweat, up the hill to the lookout where many cars park so people can view a horizon touched by boats and buoys. Turner sits down, and Spot sits beside him. His day is done. All he can think about now is his dad, the man who taught him to be well and wise. A tear starts to build on his lower eyelid as he remembers the one thing that brought him to this rock that he sits on now: *the promise.*

Spot barks at Turner as if he knows his master is lost in thought and memory. Turner gets up and starts to walk home, but Spot leads the way. He knows his home of Herring Cove.

"Where were you guys?" Sherri asks. She'd arrived home while the two friends were on their walk. She is preparing a lasagna, with extra Italian sausage and mozzarella cheese.

"Up at the lookout," Turner responds, a little sadness in his reply.

"Thinking about your dad again?"

"Yeah, a little too much today."

"Are you really going down there tomorrow?"

Sherri knows all about tomorrow. It is one of those things they talked about after they got married. Turner does not talk about it to anyone because his life, his love, everything he decided to be in this world was in some way influenced by tomorrow: *the promise.*

"Yes, I am going and you are coming with me. You have to."

"No, no, no. Not me. I have too much stuff to do." She knew this meant a lot to her husband, but she thinks it may be better if he does it alone.

"It would mean a lot if you came with me." Turner looks into Sherri's eyes in a way he never has before—more steadily and sharply, more alive and absolute than the day he said he loved her for the first time. She thought for a few seconds. Tomorrow is his day.

"Okay, I will come."

Turner smiles. He hopes for something special, some momentous inspiration in this upcoming day. They eat supper, watch television, and wind down for the evening. As they climb in bed, Spot finds himself a place at the foot of the covers. Turner looks at his family picture, particularly at his father, and closes his eyes, realizing the day has finally come. His wait is over.

2. VOYAGE

"Spot, get down, I'm awake," Turner mumbles, as the brilliant sunlight of a new day creeps through the curtain of the bedroom window. Spot sometimes wakes his master up before the alarm clock does; it is as if the canine can comprehend Atlantic Daylight Standard Time. Turner understands why people say dog is man's best friend. Dogs kiss you without asking, listen on command, and the look of love when they put their head to the side is real reason you have the adorable animal under your roof.

"You are going to do this, aren't you?" Sherri asks, finally recognizing that the day has come.

"I have to."

Turner goes to the bathroom and turns on the sink faucet. He thinks about all the patients he is supposed to see at the Abbie Lane today. Their thoughts about their relations and illnesses, about being alone in the world, about how their only friends are the pills they take every day. Turner's thoughts are so preoccupied with his job, he doesn't see what is in front of him and brushes his teeth for a full ten minutes.

"Are you all right?" Sherri asks, banging on the white wooden door.

"I hope so."

Turner finishes getting ready; he puts on a comfortable pair of shorts and a T-shirt. With hair combed and sneakers laced, he is ready to face the day he has been anticipating for a long time.

"I am ready too."

Sherri is radiant. Her lips are like mints you want to taste; her red hair is like fresh lava sliding down the mountain. Her pale face is cold, needing emotion to stir life. She is dressed in a red blouse with green cropped trousers. She resembles a flower at full bloom, never picked, bringing love to a man who does not know what fate has written.

"Maybe I should do this by myself," Turner speaks softly, wondering if this is a one-man mission.

"Maybe you should, but that would mean I got ready for nothing." Sherri smiles the smile that Turner cannot resist. Turner smiles back and knows he will not be alone today.

The couple says goodbye to Spot, as the big black dog licks their faces. They can hear him barking as they set out on their way toward Highway 103.

The two don't speak as they travel down the highway; their differences on this day maybe small but they do exist. Even though they are madly in love, they cannot read each other's minds, although at times, they sense each other's thoughts, ideas, and emotions. As they drive down the highway, no words are spoken until they enter Lunenburg County and see the sign proclaiming the area as the "Balsam Fir Christmas Tree Capital of the World."

"Christmas trees," Sherri whispers, biting her bottom lip, trying to erase a memory from her youth. The Christmas Eve had started like any other: her parents, her brother, presents, happiness. She went to bed with expectations of toys, stockings filled with candy canes, and chocolate-covered cherries. Early that winter morning, she opened her bedroom door and saw the Christmas tree in the living room in a blaze, scorching the house, turning the white ceiling into a black fury. She went to save her brother and got him out of the house, hoping her parents would save themselves. But even with all smoke detectors ringing, Sherri's parents never made it out of the house.

Sherri and her brother grew up with their aunt and uncle. Since that Christmas Day, she has believed that a good and forgiving God never existed. Perhaps now, with the father-in-law she has never met and the fulfillment of Turner's promise, there still may be a tiny hope, a speck-of-dust chance that a beneficial God exists.

"Christmas is a good thing," Turner reassures her.

"I know."

Not having many family and friends, Turner and Sherri Whynot had married under the sky, with a judge, a marriage license, and their love. They believed they didn't need a man of the cloth to consummate the will they shared in their hearts.

The two lovebirds continue down Highway 103 and turn off exit 10, entering the charm of Mahone Bay: the trinity of churches, a bay of countless islands, the stories of old boats haunting the pristine water that have made the poetic town a tourist treasure since its incorporation in 1783.

They stop at the Irving gas station at the bottom of the bay and gas up, picking up some Tim Hortons coffee at the same time.

"We gotta get there," Turner says to Sherri, anticipation flooding his face.

"I know this day is for you, but can we do something for me first?"

"Anything."

"I would like to see Lunenburg."

Though they live in the Halifax Regional Municipality, they have never seen the beauty and historical mystique of Nova Scotia's south shore. Turner has prepared for this day for so long, he wants the whole experience to be a series of firsts. Sherri's suggestion to see Lunenburg ensures that the day will be very important.

They continue their journey and enter Lunenburg; established in 1753, it is a United Nations World Heritage Site, one of only a few in Canada. The Whynots drive into the old town, welcomed by cows grazing in their pastures; the old red and white Lunenburg Academy looks down at the community, looking down on its written lineage. They make their way up Lincoln Street, the busiest shopping way in town; it is straight like most streets in the town, many of them one-way.

The fishing community is filled with widow walks homes so old that history will not let them be torn down.

The couple drives down to the Fisheries Museum of the Atlantic, where they see the boat-building barns, most painted red, as if to tell ships and their crews that this old harbor is a stopping place for rest and peace from the terror of the Atlantic Ocean. Lunenburg was the birthplace of the fastest ship of its day, the legendary *Bluenose* schooner, built in 1921.

"I would like to stay all day, but we have to get to Bridgewater," Turner says.

"Okay," Sherri answers, as she breathes in the salt from the old dory (a small wooden fishing boat) shops and the endless tales brought back from the ocean. The sea is in everything.

They leave Lunenburg and head toward Bridgewater, taking a scenic road traveled by regulars who know their way; passing by a school that seems like it does not belong; Spectacle Lakes, a settlement of the Whynots namesakes but not their kin; and finally the Lahave River, which leads to the town of Bridgewater.

"We're finally here," Turner says.

Peace takes over his body, the peace he has longed for. Bridgewater looks like a tiny Halifax, but it is more serene. They cross the old bridge and land on King Street, the street that begins Turner's rite of passage. Stopping for a moment, he pulls out the address he has looked at on the nights he thinks of his father, the address of a predestined promise. Then he continues driving along the opposite side of the Lahave River. The calm river and the sky, its sibling, bring a lull to the day. They pass by a tiny convenience store and gas station and come to the community, Pleasantville, where he will meet the man who can bring his thoughts to realization.

Turner remembers watching a movie when he was younger with his father; it was called *Pleasantville* and was one of their favorites. It was about a boy who entered a world he had always loved. Through the television into a 1950's black and white sitcom, but misses what he had left in the present. Due to his prescence, things start to change; some people want them to remain the same. But with time, revelation, color, learning, and understanding, one boy turns his world into new meaning, for the better. A black and white world turned into a colorful new life.

"Do you know where we are going?" Sherri asks.

Turner doesn't have to look at the crinkled paper he had been given long ago; he knows the address by heart. They park in the driveway; a glaze of sweat starts to form on Turner's forehead.

"Are you going to ring the doorbell, or do you want me to?" Sherri says, noticing his anxiety.

"I'll do it," Turner responds.

They walk up to the door, hand in hand, and ring the doorbell, hearing the footsteps that welcome them behind the entrance.

"Hello, can I help you?" says a blushing, beautiful, chubby woman. Her hair is gold and silver, her skin somewhat bronzed as though she had competed in her own moral Olympics and won. Her warmth begins to warm Turner, but he grasps Sherri's hand tighter.

"We are here to see Adam Jack Pelley," Turner Whynot speaks, swallowing as he does so.

3. ADAM

"He is not here." the woman responds.

Turner Whynot's throat becomes a vice, turning tighter and tighter with every second. He releases his wife's hand; his knees starting to weaken; collapse is imminent.

"Who are you?" the woman asks, her brows coming together.

Turner cannot speak; his tongue is frozen.

"My name is Sherri Whynot, and this is my husband, Dr. Turner Whynot. We were told to come here on this day, to this address, to see Adam Jack Pelley."

"You must be related to Dr. David Whynot." Realization breaks on the woman's face.

"Yes, my father," Turner says, now able to speak, knowing he is at the right place.

"Come in. I am Adam's mother, Mindy."

The couple walk in to a home that looks like any other home. Sofas, recliners, and pictures of memories that are important to the people who live there. Mindy leads them into the kitchen, where a man sits at a table, playing solitaire.

"Ray, this is Dr. Whynot's son."

Ray is an older man, balding with a streak of gray hair on his head; he wears an old golf shirt. He is the type of man who never hides his honesty, a Mason in his own right.

"Wish that man was still around," Ray snaps, as he plays one more card.

"*I'm* here," Turner responds.

Ray looks at Mindy, in a way that shows they have been waiting for the day when someone would come back to see their child. Mindy offers the Whynots a glass of water. "Like I said, Adam is not here. You know, today is his birthday. I would love to see him too, but I don't know how to get to him. Earlier this year he left, just took off. We believe he got sick again and went out to that place he always talks about. I have no clue how to get out there."

"Mindy," Turner interrupts her.

"Yes."

"It is really important for me, for us, to talk to your son. I have been looking forward to this for a long, long time. Is there any possible way we can go to this place you speak of and see Adam. Please."

"Let me get on the phone,"

Mindy can tell by the tone of his voice—now clear thanks to the water she has offered him—that Turner has a need, not merely a desire, to see her son. She picks up an old address book, looks up and dials a number, and slips into the other room, taking the phone with her.

"So you're a doctor. What kind?" Ray asks, breaking the tension of silence in the room.

"Psychiatrist, sir."

"Like your father."

"Yes, sir."

"How long?"

"Four years."

"In Halifax?"

"Yes sir, I work at the Abbie Lane building,"

"Good, maybe somebody with a head on their shoulders can talk that boy into coming back into the real world. I know Mindy will tell you the same."

Mindy comes back into the room, beaming. "Someone will be here shortly to take you to see him," she says.

Turner looks around the kitchen; a calendar with today's date, June 6, shoots into his mind. Why this day? Why his birthday? He looks over to the refrigerator and takes in the pictures of dogs and Mindy with an old friend, and a young man with a smile so curious, mystery lay between his lips. The picture that tickles Turner's fancy the most is a Polaroid of an old man pointing to the kid with the curious smile and a forehead that is red with bumps and a fresh bruise. Each man in the picture cracks a grin as if he understands something.

"Who is this man?" Turner asks Mindy, pointing to the young man in the Polaroid.

"The crazy one you're looking for," Ray interrupts, finishing another game of solitaire.

"Come here, I'll show you some more."

Mindy takes Turner and Sherri back into the living room and shows them Adam's graduation picture and other old photos. Finally, Turner can put a face to the name. They go back to the kitchen, sit, and talk about the Whynots' life, Mindy and Ray's time in Pleasantville, and how unique the calm day is. The doorbell rings.

The entrance swings open, and a man of average height and a blend of silver and black hair walks through; his goatee matches the top of his head, and freckles dot his face.

Before Mindy introduces the stranger to the Whynots, she hugs him like he is her own child, the child she wanted to see on the day she gave birth.

"Hi, Mindy,"

"Hello, Jesse."

Jesse wants to take his shoes off and stay for awhile, but sunlight is precious to him. He is a teacher in Bridgewater and a family man, and grading exams and supervising his own kid's studies make his slate full. But hearing the tone in Mindy's voice over the phone today made him realize that there was an emergency of tiny proportion. In any case of emergency someone must answer and he had to respond.

"Mindy, I would love to stay and chat, but this is a very important time for me, with work and all. Who am I takin' out there?"

"This is Turner and Sherri Whynot. Turner and Sherri, this is Jesse."

Jesse wants to shake their hands, but there will be time for introductions later.

"Let's go," Jesse says.

"Hold on." Mindy hurries into her bedroom and returns with a gift package, wrapped in red paper with a gold bow. She walks slowly; the gift is a bit heavy for her.

"We doubted any of us would see him today. Can you please give this to Adam? Please."

Adam's mother gives the gift to Turner. Her eyes begin to fill with tears, but she does not cry. They are neither tears of joy nor of sorrow, just water.

The Whynots say goodbye to their new friends, put on their shoes, and walk out to the driveway.

"You're gonna have to follow me, eh," Jesse says.

"Can we just come with you?" Turner asks, a little fearful of getting lost on his quest.

"No worries. Just follow me."

Jesse gets in to his sleek blue sedan and takes off toward the Lahave Ferry, one of only a couple of operating cable ferries in Canada. The Whynots follow, not speaking a word like when they began their trip, just holding hands, hands now becoming wet and clammy.

The ferry is waiting for them, like the captain knew they were coming. The two cars get on the ferry, the only two cars on the boat during the short voyage. Their tickets look like coupons for carnival rides. They get out of their vehicles, lean over the side of the ferry, and appreciate the serenity of the ripples on the river.

"How long have you known Adam?" Turner asks Jesse, wanting to know more than just a face in a picture frame.

"A long time," he answers, looking down at the water. Jesse seems entranced by the still, warm picture created by the Lahave River, in deep thought about something the rest of the world does not know.

"Can you tell us everything you know about Adam?"

Jesse looks at the Whynots, his eyes as peaceful as the south shore. "If I told you everything I know about my friend, would this trip you are taking today make any sense? My advice to you is talk to him, if you can."

Jesse looks back down the river, his arms folded and resting on the side of the ferry. The Whynots join him. Time passes quickly; none of them notice the ferry has docked on the other side of the river.

Jesse and the Whynots jump in their cars. Jesse leads and the questioning couple follow. The two follow the blue car through a series of nice, little communities, the town of Riverport, villages with views of beaches guarded by large, grassy cliffs. They finally arrive in Kingsburg and drive up a steep, rocky road. It leads them to a small lot where cars were never supposed to be.

Jesse gets out of his car and grabs a paper bag. "Please give this to Adam," he says.

"You're not coming with us?" Sherri's eyes grow with bewilderment.

"I told myself I would never go out there again. Today is no different." Jesse not only extends his hand, he embraces them both. He has brought them to the place he will never forget, the place he thinks about often. "Could you give this to him, and tell him I said hello," Jesse asks, handing a shiny brown bag to Sherri.

"How do we reach him? Where do we go?" Turner says, lost in a wilderness that is unknown, a wild that is yet to be read by the world.

"The path is that way," are Jesse's departing words. He points toward a trail made by hikers' feet, then gets in his car and drives, slowly, down the stone road.

"You still wanna do this?" Sherri asks her husband.

"I have to."

Turner grabs the red present from the car while Sherri holds the gift from Jesse. The more they hike, the more beautiful Rose Bay becomes.

The rose: the petal of promise, the thorn of thought, the flower of forgiveness. On the opposite side of the bay are striking cliffs aged by the natural progressive struggle with the sea to maintain their edge. "The Ovens," as they are called, allow everyone to see this battle. The old path's history is told by roots and moss, branches, seaweed and sand brought forth from the Atlantic Ocean. The path looks as if it had been used with frequency long ago, but now nature seems to want to cover it over, to say that no one should travel it anymore.

Turner and Sherri follow the woven edge, the path that does not go into the wood, staying close to new plants and jagged cliff. An aged tree inhibits their way, its fall caused by the force of the shore. Turner climbs over, and Sherri ducks under; they continue walking. Over one more hill, they come upon a cabin, small and quaint. They are so far out, at a point of no return; the inevitable questions form in their minds. How could this cabin get here? Who would build this? Why? With all questions, they do finally have their answer. A dwelling, a habitat, life. Adam.

Flying from the cabin is the Nova Scotia flag, the blue X with the golden arms of Scotland and a Scottish lion in the middle. The flag barely catches the breeze off the bay.

"Do you think we should go in?" Sherri asks his husband.

"I was going to ask you the same thing."

"Jesse said keep following the path."

The path leads past the cabin and through some old petrified trees, up to rolling moss hills, overlooking silent waves and more rugged cliffs. Sitting on the green, hands on knees, all senses focusing back on the horizon, the sun focusing back on him, is one man. They know it is Adam. They approach and introduce themselves.

"Hello, sir. My name is Dr. Turner Whynot. This is my wife Sherri. We are here to see Adam Jack Pelley. Are you him?" Turner speaks formally because he is nervous, with chills coursing through his blood and spine, hair and limbs. He almost drops the red birthday gift.

"Yup," Adam responds.

Adam is of average height, with a husky build and shoulders on which he can carry the sky. He has a bushy beard, long hair, a straight forward nose, and a mysterious smile. He wears a Boston Red Sox baseball cap with peanut butter smudged on the bill and brown-rimmed glasses. His brow creates a slight shadow over his eyes, as if the love that created him wants to hide his soul. His khaki pants and hooded navy sweatshirt are dirty; they seem to be the only clothes he has worn for weeks.

Turner's throat starts to constrict again, but he is still able to speak. "We were told to find you here, but I've been wondering, why here?"

Adam turns his focus from the blue of his peaceful world, seeing his new companions' faces for the first time. "Waiting," he says, his greenish eyes looking into Turner's own.

"Waiting for what?"

"Waiting," Adam replies. He turns back to the blue. The Whynots look at the horizon with him. Minutes go by; finally, Adam speaks, again.

"You must be related to Dr. David Whynot."

"Yes, he was my father."

Adam nods his head, stands up, and brushes off some old twigs. "You saw the cabin on your way here."

"Yes," Turner acknowledges.

"Lead the way," Adam gestures with his hand.

The trio walk back to the cabin and enter through an old door with rusty hinges. Inside is an old cast-iron stove. Turner thinks there is no way a man could have transported this heavy black appliance to this part of the earth, no matter what device was used. Impossible. There is a table on which to eat, a bench cupboard for storing things, and a loft in which a man can dream.

"What brought you here?" Adam asks.

"Jesse," Turner responds.

"No, I mean, what brought you here?"

"I think I was supposed to make this trip today."

"Huh ... What's in the bag?"

Adam has an idea what is in the red package; he knows his mother's gifts. Only his mother would wrap something that way. Sherri passes Adam the brown paper bag. He pulls out two magazines. One is a World Wrestling Entertainment publication with John Cena on the cover. The title says "The Champ Is Here!"

"Cool," Adam says, with curiosity in his mysterious smile. He looks at the other magazine. It is a basketball publication called *Slam*. On the cover is LeBron James. The title says simply, "The King."

"Cool," Adam says again, mystery in his curious smile. He flips through the *Slam* magazine as the Whynots stare at him attentively. "What do you want to know?" he says, abruptly.

"Everything," the Whynots say simultaneously.

"I will tell you my truth, why I am here, my life, my illness. This day, my birthday, is the start of my story. You are here because of your father; I am here because I know. This may take a while, but I promise you will be out of here by the time the sun goes down. I would like to offer you a coffee, but I don't have any. If you would like something to drink, I will open my package.

The Whynots watch in anticipation as Adam opens Mindy's gift. Inside is bread, peanut butter, cans of soup, toilet paper, juice, and diet Pepsi. A mother's care package.

Adam pours Turner and Sherri a drink and begins his story. A story of patience. A story of a sinner. Just a story.

4. KING PELLES

"Where do we start?" Turner asks. He had thought that Adam would be taller, more intimidating. He doesn't know whether to speak to him as a patient or as someone without mental illness. Sherri is trying to find something real in Adam through his mystical eyes, trying to understand the man in front of her, trying to understand the day.

"There was a beginning to where we sit, a place where our ancestors fought for purpose and dreams. A kingdom ruled for worship and service. The ocean, the once last frontier, the place where all things were supposed to end became the origin of all wonder, the answer to what we know. The tale of kings and courage, a tale of belief through vision. Just like your trip today, there also must have been a primary voyage."

Adam looks out of the small window in the cabin, his sight skipping over the sea to the land of myth, the land of Camelot.

"Let this knight put thy sword through so you can see our God," Sir Gawaine whispered into the Pict's ear, as he dropped to his knees drawing in his last breath. The sun was directly above him. At noon, he was stronger than any of the enemy he faced. It was a small attack by an obscure band of savages, dirty with tattoos; there must have been lunacy in their minds for them to think they could take the kingdom of Camelot. With bodies slain, Picts and the few true warriors of King Arthur's court, the surviving men of Camelot, knelt down on one knee, looking over the horror, and took off their helmets and shields to make peace and prayer for what just had occurred.

"Why do we slay these faces we have never seen, not even knowing their names, if they have family?" A young man of the infantry shivered, not understanding the scene around him.

Sir Gareth stood up and planted his sword in the ground. "I have journeyed all across this land, with shield and sword, ready to battle for my king and the blood of my children. But when I see death in the eyes of another from my sword and when I see my child born, I serve my king with everything I have learned because if I serve my king, than I serve my God and the grail."

"We will protect Camelot, King Arthur, and all that be, my brother Gareth," said Sir Gawaine. "Camelot is our home, where stories have come to tell us to honor truth, the truth that has lived and died for all. Some honor truth by making garments as gifts; we honor truth by our sword." Sir Gawaine looked at the young infantryman in his eyes. The knights knew it was his first battle and that it wouldn't be his last. "Am I right, good hands? What do you say, my brother in arms and blood?"

"Mount up. Off to Camelot," Sir Gareth commanded, in a gentle and courteous tone that was surprising given that he'd just been in battle.

A black hawk with sharp talons flew over the men, observing the result of the battle. The sky was lonely, with few clouds, making the bird feel close to the presence of God, the wind in its wings making it feel closer to Jesus. The hawk had a twig in his mouth, a sign of something to come. He flew low across the rolling fields of green, which looked like ocean waves, then came high over a wild river and entered Camelot. The hawk flew over peasants in sheep's clothing while the merchants who had sold the garments wore valuable tunics made of silk. Fowl and rabbit for food, liquor and fine grass for the mind. Bagpipes blew—the sound of the land. All men were gentlemen, except for a few thieves and those who quarreled over love that was lost. The hawk was hungry, and he could not perch anywhere or find a nest to fill his needs. He landed behind a store, and in a magical shift became a mouse small enough to sneak into any house and eat enough crumbs to fill its belly. After eating some nuts and some apple skins, he picked up the twig again, went in and out of small holes, and came to an opening. From there, he could see the two knights of the Round Table, Sir Gawaine and Sir Gareth, and their warriors ride back into Camelot, applause following them.

The knights jumped off their saddles and entered the cathedral, ready to report the battle to his majesty, King Arthur. The mouse snuck in, nipping his tail between the cathedral doors just before they closed. As they entered, all the other knights were around the Round Table. Gawaine and Gareth took their swords, covered in dry blood, and put them on the table, as all of the other knights had already done. All the knights were present.

The doors opened again, and the exalted one entered the room: King Arthur.

"My men, how are thee?"

"Our battle went well, sire, only a few casualties."

"Let those men be in the arms of God, and sit with the others who have fought for Camelot and the Grail. Now then, we must eat for those men who have returned. Macdonald!"

A man wearing a red cloak with a yellow sash came into the room, smiling,

"Prepare a feast for my noble knights!"

"Yes, Your Majesty."

Macdonald exited, and before King Arthur could speak again, Sir Gawaine said, "My King, I have fought in your service so long I have lost sense of time. Chivalry is my being. I believe that our one true God watches us through all our battles. But we have been always sworn to secrecy to protect one thing—the Grail, the cup of Jesus. Yet I do not believe any of your selected knights have ever seen the chalice."

Gawaine now remembered the young warrior on the battle field; why would he fight a man without knowing his name?

"Does it matter if you see the Grail, or do you need to see it to believe in our God?" Arthur asked.

The knights were silent, looking down at the table, knowing they would not fight or even dress if they did not believe. Finally, the simple righteous knight spoke. "I know of the Holy Grail and of someone who saw it," Galahad said.

Everyone looked at Galahad. Arthur, with a grin on his face, was holding his chin,

"My grandfather, King Pelles, had it all—land, water, a castle, a kingdom. He did not go to the Grail; it came to him. He was a guardian of the Grail; it filled his body with bliss no word can explain. Then in battle a mystic sword wounded him, and since then he can hardly move, can hardly do anything. He looked to the stars for answers; his dreams are more real than the kingdom he once knew. He is in his own reality, though his reality is a wasteland. He lives in his castle, Carbonek, and goes to fish. He never catches anything, but he will still fish. Ever since the Grail, that battle, he has not been the same. This is my grandfather, King Pelles."

"Who is your father, Galahad?" King Arthur asked. The king knew everything about most of his knights but his sense of Galahad that he was so pure and valid, trust would be a word unvalued.

"I do not know."

"I do."

"Stand, Lancelot," King Arthur said.

Sir Lancelot was the greatest knight of the round table and one of the king's most heralded friends. But through the temptation of skin and the sins of seduction, he had betrayed what he believed in most.

"My King," Lancelot said. "I love you like my brother, like we were from the same mother. But there is a mist in my eyes, a feeling I cannot resist. I have laid down with Guinevere, your beautiful queen. If I wish to do it again I will, but I will still ask for forgiveness. This King Pelles you speak of used some spell, tricked me to think that his daughter was your lady, and I ask again to forgive my oath and loyalty. Galahad, you are my child. Arthur, I am your knight."

Arthur's face began to shake. He drew his sword, and his knights picked up their own. If the king could not trust his most faithful knight, how could any knight trust each other? The only one who stood still was Galahad, who was in wonder. Then he began to speak,

"What are you all looking for? A cup that had our lord's blood in it? I, too, would like to drink from it, to hold it. But if you want the Grail, the true holy blood, it is here." Galahad pointed to his heart with his index finger, the organ pumping fast, making his blood run. "And here." Galahad pointed to the center of his body with his index finger; his soul, the energy from his aura poured through the cathedral. "Without this, there would be no Grail. Fight each other or defend what we have defended for so long."

A wind started to swirl in the room. The mouse that had made his way through the door started to get bigger and bigger, finally turning into a short man with a fluorescent black cloak, a beard down to his breast, eyes of every color. The twig the mouse was holding now turned into a branch.

"Merlin," Arthur said, still holding his sword.

"There is no need for war in a cathedral. There must be peace within these walls."

All the knights put their swords down and sat in their seats.

"I see you are looking for the chalice of Christ," Merlin said, his voice cracking with every syllable.

"You know of it, Merlin?" Arthur said.

"Yes, but now it is not of this world."

"Continue."

"The carpenter's cup has gone past the ends of the earth to another world, to a place not touched by man. It is protected by inlets of sand, a puzzle of islands, trees of oak, tides that run so fast boats become shipwrecked in minutes. It is marked by a river, like the one here by Camelot, but it is made of gold. It is buried so well that it may never see sky again. Rocks mark the island where it lies; rocks mark where it stays. But there lies a black magic over the land, and only the righteous of righteousness may hold the treasure once again. Let this branch bring peace to you and to Camelot."

"What should we do, Merlin?" asked the king.

"Do what you have done: fight for your God, keep this secret, and pray for those who have nothing. Now, is there anything to eat?"

The knights laughed as Macdonald came into the room. Pieces of meat with bread, ale, and a new Macdonald favorite, potatoes cut in the style of fingers. The knights ate. They were filled with food and spirit. Galahad rose and picked up his sword; pointing it to the middle of the table, he said, "To life, to love, to the king."

Lancelot rose, "No, my son. To the Grail, to a new world."

All the knights rose and saluted, "To a new world."

The knights drank more, wondering if someone, someday would drink out of the Grail. A new world, a frontier that once was thought to be the end of all creation, begins the story about the resting place to the question of the knight's vision and legacy. An answer to the resting place of a pirates dream.

5. JACK

"Where is this place you speak of?" Turner asks, mesmerized by the young man's eyes. Sherri is not so impressed.

"An old sea hand told me about a man who was looking for treasure beyond any value of gold or silver," says Adam. "A treasure that would make the man who found it a legend. The old hand said the man looked fatigued, as if he'd had this booty on his mind his whole life, never escaping his spirit. The man had traveled everywhere, searching, finally resting in Halifax, convinced the treasure was buried on the shores of Nova Scotia.

"Where do you think it is?" Turner's interest is piqued, his mouth is wide.

Adam doesn't answer; he just glances at Turner and Sherri.

John Rackham, known as Calico Jack, had not slept for days. The demonic laughs of evil, shipwrecked sailors echoed through his head. All he could do was drink. The boats off the coast of Jamaica that his crew had plundered in the name of piracy gave them little gold but lots of liquor. Rum. The rum soothed the body but allowed the laughing to continue.

While looking at his journal to find the location of the next booty, he caught a glimpse of his face in an empty rum bottle. Jack rushed to a cracked mirror by his bed. Panic started to spread in his soul, maybe a soul he didn't have. In the mirror he saw his nice, white calico shirt (a fine garment from India), striped pants, a black wig he had not taken off for days, and his eyes—one so far open you could see the universe with it, the other closed so tightly it couldn't possibly see anything.

Jack knew that if his crew saw his eyes, a sinister face like this, there would be mutiny aboard his ship, the *William*. Everyone aboard the fast sloop, and pretty much all men who became sailors, had nothing at sea except memories of home and a God that will guide them. If Jack's sailors saw his eyes, they would believe that evil was steering the course, that no good wind would catch their canvas. Not even his beautiful quartermasters would stand behind him.

Jack had gone from pardon to partner. He'd been to Providence to seek a pardon for a quarrel. There, he met a woman named Anne Bonny who wanted to leave her marriage because there was no happiness at home. The two came together, and the *William* was born.

Pirates: the sinners of sea, the order of ocean, the trick of treasure.

They manipulated the Caribbean for years, with many mates on board, including one who was very tenacious, hungry for more. Anne Bonny saw this unusual buccaneer and advanced, scantily dressed, only to finding out it was not a "he" but a "she," Mary Read. Instead of killing her or throwing her off the boat, Anne became her friend, helping Jack to find riches and seeing what the new world could offer the *William*.

Under a wooden chest of maps, Jack found an old eye patch. He didn't use the patch the way other pirates did. He was a natural navigator, and his eyes adjusted to the light and dark of the day easily. He spent most of his time in front of the sky rather than underneath the deck. The patch fit, but he didn't want to wear it. He knew that when his crew saw the patch on his face they'd know that something was wrong, that something was different about their captain. Calico Jack felt emergency in his body along with the evil voices. A drastic thought entered his mind.

It was time to go to the upper deck, above the captain's quarters, to see the day. It was glorious, with few clouds and even a rainbow to match the cloths around the shoulders and waists of some of the men. Jack waited for the question.

"What happened to your eye?" Anne Bonny asked, quite concerned.

"I woke up, and something was wrong."

"What?"

"I think it is the light," Jack lied, trying to convince them there was nothing laughing in his head. He looked down the deck. Given his morning reflection and now what he saw through his one eye, it had to be done,

"Boatswain!" Jack called.

"Yes, sir,"

"I know some of our mates sleep under our map, the stars the lord has given. But we keep this ship clean, and if we don't ..." Calico Jack drew his pistol and shot the boatswain, a look of death and disbelief coming over the now-soon-to-be ghost of pirate tales.

"We must keep this ship clean, so we can catch our coin, our rubies, our rum. Keep her clean, and all of us will have treasure. What is your name?" Jack points at a young and colorful mate, a single gold hoop in his ear.

"Luke, sir,"

"My mates, Luke is our new boatswain. If he does his job, gold will come to him; if not, I will load my pistol again."

Everyone went to work: riggings, cleaning, setting guns and cannons for battle. Luke cleaned the deck, and the rest of the crew threw the old boatswain overboard. Because of the death of the boatswain, no one noticed the eye patch over Calico Jack's face.

"Captain, ship ahead," said the mate from the crow's nest, only one warning sight from the unusually large sloop.

Jack put his pistol in the air." Men, let's do what the sea tells us. Prepare the boat to invade this ship. Bring her flag down."

With the *William*'s flag flying high, a black flag with skull and two cutlass swords below, the men loaded their handheld weapons with powder and filled their cannons so they could crush the merchant ship. Before that ship could prepare itself, the *William* turned broadside, facing the side of its victim, and fired everything within its cannons, destroying the defenseless ship. Splinters and wood chips were buried deep into the merchant sailors' bodies, sending some of those sailors of the merchant ship into the spirit of the sea.

"Let us come about and board," Jack ordered. His sailing master had the *William* come about and dock it next to the merchant ship, tying their vessel to what was left of the other.

"Who is your captain?" Calico Jack asked, throwing himself on top of the yard arm.

"He was wounded by your cannon and then passed in my arms," said a man wearing a blood-stained orange and blue sweater. "I am his quartermaster."

"What is in your hold, quartermaster?"

The quartermaster knew he could not hide what was in the merchant ship, only maybe the few coins in his pocket.

"Tea, silk, and so much rum and gold I cannot count."

Mary and Anne looked at each other and smiled. They loved fine clothes, they loved to drink, but the ladies really loved their gold.

"Thank you, sir. We will take it all. You can keep your flag. Now, I have a proposition for you who have survived; I give you quarter, and you can join my crew, share my riches. But if you do not join the crew of the *William*, I will hang you from this yardarm."

The quartermaster was the only one survivor; he joined the *William*'s crew. They were so satisfied with the take, the loot, that they decided to rest and get their land legs back. A couple more days of the tossing, and they would find a quiet port.

All of the mates, even the new boatswain, Luke, were in the captain's quarters, drinking the fine Jamaican rum they had relieved from the now-forgotten merchant ship. "Today, my friends, we shall drink to all our buccaneers who have died on the deep, and those who have become rich on the rise. Drink the rum, wear the fine silk. There will be many more ships to sink, but our *William* will ride the mercy of the tide forever." Calico Jack bellowed.

The crew of the William cheered, toasted, and drank more. They drank so much, Calico Jack forgot he was looking out of one eye. The crew was so drunk, they still didn't notice the leather patch.

"John, could you please come up to the deck." Anne Bonny called to Calico Jack below; it was a tender call.

"My crew, I must now attend to the finer points in life. The rum does not now call me as much as the lips of the ladies." Jack put his cup down and started to stagger up the stairs. He could still hear those voices laughing, jumping inside of his head, but the ladies would help him ignore them. He did not have one lady on his mind, but two; this was a night where three would come together.

"Hello, Calico Jack."

A man with a blue jacket, white cuffs, white pants, and a black military hat had a huge grin on his face and his hands behind his back. The rest of his men, about seventy-five of them, stood behind him with their muskets drawn. Anne Bonny and Mary Read stood next to Calico Jack, hand in hand, their clothes and hair loose and ragged as if they had put up a fierce but futile fight to save the ship and their way of life.

"Calico Jack, or should I say John Rackham, I am Captain Barnet, and I captain this governor's ship for the French army and its king, Louis XV. You are hereby arrested for piracy and treason. We will take you and your crew to Port Royal, where you will be tried to see if you will be hung." Barnet's grin told Jack there was nothing he could do.

The ladies looked like they were about to cry. Jack was so drunk he thought he was dreaming. Finally, Calico Jack knew it was over; he took the patch off of his head and threw it on the deck, drinking back his last bit of rum.

"Take me you cursed sea, take me," he said, and the French regiment took Calico Jack, Mary Read, Anne Bonny, Luke the boatswain, the crew and the *William* into custody.

Sitting in a Port Royal jail cell, Calico Jack's eyes still did not change. Inmates were scared at the sight of him. He sat in the corner, picturing the rope, the noose. Boatswain Luke was near him, not saying anything, not wondering about the noose but what was beyond it.

"Come here," Jack said to Luke.

Luke slid his way over, hands and ass on the ground; without any rum in him, he was a little scared of Jack.

"Luke, I will see the gallows, but you, being so young, may escape with your life. So, I will tell you a secret that my tongue has not spoken since a wise pirate told it to me. North, way north from here, is where all pirates point their flags. Most pirates search for gold and rubies, for treasure. But all pirates want to be remembered until the sea stops moving. I have been told of rivers of gold, more gold that you can dream, but this treasure is the way of all man. And it is settled and found by oak, marked simply, but buried so well it is like many games that are hard to win. Go north, find a quiet port that knows of this island. From there, let your quest begin."

The jail door opened; it was time for sentencing.

"John Rackham, let's go."

"Remember, Luke, all men."

Luke sat in his cell and waited for his sentence. He did not hang. They released him to be a boatswain on a small French ship. The colder it got on ship, the more Luke thought about Calico Jack. "All men," he said. Luke thought his purpose in life would not be complete until he made it north someday.

6. DISCOVER

A dam walks out of the cabin to pee. Sherri wipes her nose and wonders why she walked out here. "This guy is crazy! He's talking about knights and pirates."

"Give him some time. There is a reason why we are out here," Turner replies. Sherri doesn't know Adam, but she trusts her husband.

"There was once a story told to me about a boy who discovered what we know today as the most famous treasure site of all time, Oak Island." Adam says walking back into the cabin. "But this boy also discovered something within himself, something maybe all should discover."

Bub woke up at the crack of dawn and saw that the moon had made the skyline red, as though it had painted the horizon the night before. Bub was an only child, so responsibilities around his farm were more demanding than his games with friends down the road. He thought the quicker things got done, the more fun he'd have with friends at Western Shore, near Mahone Bay.

He did what he had to do. He looked after cattle, fed livestock, and cleaned the barn—anything he could do to make his parents proud. Although Bub did have access to a new school that had just opened a couple of miles down the road, he was needed at home, and he understood that. His mother read him poetry and passages from the Bible. He could not read well, but he was not totally illiterate.

"Bub, soup for lunch," his mother called as he just finished his chores around the family farm for the day. He and his parents sat to a fine soup, even though their provisions were becoming scarce.

"Bub, I am getting the horses ready," his father said, "going into Mahone Bay for food and things we need. You must stay and look after your mother. I think you will do well."

"Yes, I will protect the farm," Bub said, firmly shaking his father's hand.

The horses and small carriage rode off, leaving Bub and his crying mother.

"It's okay, Mom. Let's go inside." Bub and his mother sat at the table where they ate and prayed together. All chores had been done for the day, even though it was quite early, probably because of the silent sky. "Bub," his mother said, "go, see your friends. They should be home by now. You deserve it for all the hard work you put in on the farm."

Bub was ecstatic to hear his mother's words. He ran to get a wool sweater, his knife, and his boots. Running out the door, he heard her caring voice. "Be back for supper," his mother yelled. He started down the road toward his friend's place. It would take a long time to go down the road, but he knew a short cut through a small wood. He wanted to get there fast. He took the short cut. He picked up a large branch, his staff of support, and continued down the path.

In one blink, he saw a magnificent deer, tall, with a light-brown coat and a white tail. It was chewing on some leaves. Bub stopped. He thought if he could take a deer home to his parents, enough to feed on for weeks, pride would be in all who raised him.

All Bub had was his knife, so it would be hard to catch the deer. He would have to sneak to get his steak. His footsteps were very soft on the ground, taking him almost next to the deer, but then the white tail sprinted into the thick wood, breaking branches and boughs. Bub had to make a decision, the friend or the deer.

His father liked deer steak. He left the path and followed the deer, branches scratching his skin, tripping over old roots, sometimes the wood so thick he could not see. He just kept running, running for a parent's appreciation.

Bub came to the shore; a small island was about fifty yards away, shallow water separating the two. The deer waited on the small coast and made eye contact with him. Bub knew he wanted deer meat for supper. He ran after the deer, and the animal jumped in the water, swimming over to the island.

Bub was hungry. The more he thought about the food, the more he thought about his family. Maybe they could use their scarce savings for something else. He jumped in the water, which was cold, shrinking all his pores on a May afternoon. As he crawled onto the island, there was no sign of the deer. No footprints, no sign of any animal life. He looked carefully behind every oak, always thinking that the deer was right behind the next oak tree. He hunted around the whole island until he came to a clearing on the other side. Bub could taste the venison in his mouth, see it on his family's plate.

There stood the deer, by a tackle box hanging from an oak-tree branch. There was nothing for the deer to eat, no fresh water, just a tackle box.

"Here is my chance," Bub said to himself. He walked closer and closer to the deer, but the deer did not move. He took out his knife and walked closer; still, the deer did not move. The closer he went to the deer, the more peace and tranquility lifted Bub away from the thought of the knife. As Bub walked closer, love made him throw the knife away. He walked to about an arm's length away from the white-tailed deer, which turned its head and looked him in the face.

He touched the deer, and bliss came over him, throughout his body as they stood under the pulley and rope. Bub turned around and looked at all of the islands in the bay, wondering when those islands would be discovered. Then he remembered his mother's call about supper. The deer would not be coming home with him. The treasure that Bub found within himself was where the real hunt for the pirate's treasure took place many years later. The motivation for all is what is on this island. The quest is not only about what, but where.

7. ROBERT RESTALL

"This treasure hunt has been going on for decades, continued both by presidents and men who have lost not just fortunes but their lives." Adam picks up the basketball magazine bought for him by his friend, Jesse, and opens the bottle of pop. "One day was more tragic than any other on the island," he continues. "A day long ago when many went into the darkness, never to experience the light of love ever again."

Turner is glad to have met Adam, curious as he is about the past. Sherri starts to feel this may have been a mistake; she is no longer searching but thinks now that this man may be mad.

He sat in his leather seat, looked out the window, hands behind his head. The thirty-second president of the United States of America, Franklin Delano Roosevelt, was tired but not because of his work as the leader of his country. His age was starting to slow him. It soon would be time for someone else to head the world. Despite his accomplishments as a leader, and some failures, as he thought about overcoming the Great Depression or the tragedy of Pearl Harbor, he wanted to be young again.

When he was twenty-one, he was on the western shore of Nova Scotia, digging shafts and holes, searching for something so extravagant that dimes and nickels would be forgotten in his pockets. After several months of digging, there was no treasure, nothing, Franklin Roosevelt returned to the United States, where destiny would turn him into one of the most important men on the planet.

Now he thought about the coins, the loot, that treasure chest that had to be at Oak Island. There had to be something more.

"Excuse me, sir," an intern called.

Franklin didn't hear her; he was still thinking about how he came from searching for old pirate's booty to the halls of political power.

"Excuse me, sir," the intern called again.

"Franklin." Eleanor, his wife, interrupted, quietly calling his name.

"Yes," he said, spinning around in his chair.

"Are you okay?" Eleanor asked.

"Fine."

"What were you thinking?"

"Fool's gold, honey, fool's gold."

Robert Restall was ready—just as he had been yesterday and hopefully would not need to be tomorrow—to put an end to the most famous treasure hunt in history, the Oak Island legend. With his big ears and Brylcreem hair, he had a nose that could sniff out secrets and a will that would not cease until he did. He put on a white shirt and brown trousers, ready to find fame and fortune at the same time.

Since 1795, people and money investing groups had excavated different parts of Oak Island, particularly the "money pit," called that because so much money had been wasted on the digs. In 1959, Robert moved to Oak Island with his family. For five years, he had searched for the treasure, without ever finding a penny. But Robert never gave up hope.

August 17, 1965 was hot and humid. The heat would float off the sand, making it look like jewels dancing on the sea.

"Right behind you, Dad," Bobby yelled. Robert's son was just as excited as his father to find treasure, but five years of nothing had started to make him wonder if this island were nothing more than trees and sand. "Dad, are you sure there is something here? I mean why dig here? Why dig here at all?"

"Bobby, when this chest of treasure is found, this island will be remembered until history is forgotten. I know it is here."

"Are you sure?"

"We just have to keep digging."

They walked to a dig site fifty feet away from the money pit in one direction and Smith's Cove in the other. Robert noticed that the hole had filled with some water, black and murky. He decided to turn on the mechanical pump on to remove some of the water. The invisible death (carbon monoxide produced by the pump) started its work.

"Hey, boys!" Robert yelled, as he saw Cyril Hiltz, a young teenager, and Carl Graezer, Robert's excavating partner, arrive to work on the dig for the day.

The invisible death grew more and more, taking over the pit. Robert took the initiative and started the day himself. "I'm going to go down into the pit to see how we are doing," he said. The men acknowledged him as they continued to work with their tools. The invisible death was ready to take its first victim.

Several minutes later, after building the support for another shaft, Bobby put down his tools. He hadn't heard from his father in a couple minutes. "I'm going to check on Dad," he said to the others. He went down the ladder to check on his father. He was never heard from again. The invisible death had now taken two lives.

When the Restalls did not return, Cyril and Carl ran up to the hole and saw them lying motionless in the black water at the bottom of the pit. Carl had invested so much time and effort into this Oak Island venture, he had to try to save his investment partner and his son. They were also his closest friends. Carl went down the ladder and after a few breaths, the invisible death had taken one more.

Cyril didn't know what to do; his mind and life were now in a death pit. He rushed down the ladder; the invisible death caught him and took him into the black with the others.

Another treasure hunter, Andy Demont, saw the men go down the pit and not come up. Something had to be done. He rushed over to the pit. "Anyone, anyone please help!" Andy yelled with urgency. Campers on the island started to rush over to the pit as Andy started down the ladder. The invisible death would take anyone it could. It seemed Andy was next. He fell into the pit, overcome by the fumes.

Camping on the island was Ed White, a firefighter captain by trade, who was visiting from New York. He realized that everyone in the pit had been overcome by fumes. With help from other campers, he tied a rope around himself and went down the hole, saving the unconscious Andy Demont. The other men in the black water, consumed by the invisible death, could not be saved.

On the island that day, the treasure hunt had taken four lives. One more would die later. Whatever was buried at Oak Island was not supposed to be dug up again.

"From the top of the world, a president intrigued by a tale, to the bottom of the world, a dark pit consuming life without care—this island is the beginning of my world, the place where my parents became one." Adam tells his story while he leafs through the issue of *Slam*. He opens the door to let a soft and soothing sea breeze come into the cabin. Turner gets more comfortable in his seat while Sherri looks out the window. She thinks about leaving, but she can see how interested her husband is in Adam. She thinks of her heart, her husband, and continues listening to Adam.

8. THE WEDDING

We were swimming in the pool, seeing who could hold their breath the longest. I could do the best cannonball. My cousins, young friends, and I were at the Oak Island Inn, a camera shot away from that legendary treasure pit. This was not my first visit to the Inn, but it was my most memorable. Tomorrow my parents would be married. My friends got in the hot tub, but it was too hot for me, so I looked out the window at the scenery, where treasures were dreamed and lives were taken.

The night before the marriage, a union before God, the pool could have been filled with every type of liquor imaginable. The only swimming my relatives and their friends did was between their lips and down their throats. There was no drowning of sorrows; it was a celebration of the future and more liquor-filled days of happiness to come.

The day had come, causing many headaches. The males who were important to my dad were ready to share this day. Dad's pinstriped navy-blue suit and red tie made him the best-dressed man at the inn. He was a little nervous; he had been married before. He was a radio celebrity, whose job was playing the music he knew and loved. Whenever I was with my dad and someone heard his voice, that person would blush and smile.

"You're Jack Pelley."

"Yes, how are you?"

My father loved his music. He wanted to share it with everyone. He traveled the Maritime provinces as a DJ, playing Newfoundland music. That night, there was music.

My grandfather, Kelly Burgess, my mother's father, loved my dad, so he loved this moment. "Come here," Granddad said. "Today, you and I have to give your mother away. We have to give permission so that your dad can marry her. So when the reverend asks, 'Who gives this woman away?' I will squeeze your hand, then we will say 'I do.'"

"Okay, Granddad," I said, not knowing what giving away my mother meant.

We all went down to the lobby, the place of the ceremony. Dad and his ushers were by the fireplace; the sofas and chairs had been moved. Friends and family circled around, from the upper level down to where my mother would make her entrance.

Marriage: the bond of beliefs, the connection of course, the love of love.

She entered from the hotel hall. Sparkling. A silk, cream-colored, two-piece suit. She was shaking a bit, and then when she looked at me, the shake turned to a shiver.

My mother's maid of honor was Betty. My father's best man was Raymond. They are my godparents. They live a short drive from Oak Island. I was baptized in an Anglican church not far from their house. Many summers, I would go to their place, swim in their pool, play video games, and eat toasted cheese sandwiches cut diagonally. They are hearts with trust running through their veins. I could not think of anyone else being my godparents.

The reverend proceeded with the marriage ceremony. Standing behind Mom, all I could hear was sniffing and sniveling. All I could think about was my part.

"Who gives away this woman to this man?"

"I do," I said.

Granddad squeezed my hand after I spoke.

"I do."

As a boy, I felt happy and proud that I remembered my part but remorseful and sad that I didn't do it together with Granddad.

"You may be seated," the reverend said to Granddad and me.

I jumped on the sofa, elbows on the backrest, hands cupping my face, to watch my parents come together. My dad was stiff, like an oak on the famous island, but one that had been cut down; even leaves moved in the wind. He was still. Mom was crying; her makeup created black tears that fell down her face and made her eyes red.

Mom worked at National Sea Products in Lunenburg, She packed frozen fish, which was shipped around the world. Dad was usually on the road doing what he loved; it was mostly just me and Mom. To this day, they are my best friends.

Mom cried so much it was all I noticed during the wedding. She would look at me and smile, cry, then focus back on the reverend. I thought she was happy. Maybe I didn't understand.

They kissed, they were together, and they were one.

Everyone ate sandwiches and sweets. The celebration of my mother with a new name and a unique type of music that was loved by all at this wedding went on into the night.

Children were not allowed to be with the parents and the music that night, so I went to bed. All the people there continued to swim in liquor on this day of happiness and desire for my parents. I looked out my window and saw that the sea and the sky had created a purple peace to acknowledge their union. That was one of the last times I ever saw them get along. If it wasn't for me, I don't think there would have been a wedding. I believe they got married because of me. I believe everybody at the Oak Island Inn that day loved me. That love carried me from home to school, to new friends and a teacher that taught in her own unique way. It was also the first time that I ever felt different.

9. THE SHOE

"Duck!"

I turned around to see a red high-heel shoe shuttling to hit me right between the eyes. I threw my right arm over my face; the teacher's shoe missed me and hit the corner of one of the desks behind me, missing the classmate she was aiming at.

"How many times have I told you? I am losing the patience I have. You better smarten up and be quiet, or the other shoe is coming off. Now sit down and be quiet!"

Mrs. Goodyear, my primary and grade one elementary school teacher, was strict. All the other students said she was a "bad" teacher, maybe because her rules were not what they wanted. Mrs. Goodyear showed us that as children you might get your desires at home, but in school, it was time to learn that needs and wants are different things.

"Now, get back to your mathematics until the lunch bell. No recess until your math is done."

Mrs. Goodyear picked up her red shoe, struggling to put it on because it was too small. She looked sternly at the student at whom she'd thrown the shoe. She looked at me and smiled.

I always got along with Mrs. Goodyear. The first day of school, when my mother and I met her for orientation, it seemed that she knew me, was fascinated about me. She asked me to do a painting about anything I wanted, so I did the only thing I knew how to paint, my home, the community of Stonehurst.

Recess was always great. As a little boy, I sat on the swings and watched the older children play soccer. I always wanted to play, but I knew I could not, and I knew they would not let me play. Aaron was always on the field, commanding the play of the ball. He was one of Stonehurst's older children. Aaron hardly ever missed school, and he never missed soccer at recess.

The buzzer rang, ending recess and signaling the beginning of classes for the afternoon. Most afternoons, Mrs. Goodyear read stories to her primary classes, stories based on moral values that we should share with loved ones and keep for lifetimes. Children's stories are the best stories. I always sat at the back of the class, so I could either look at my classmates or pick my nose without anyone noticing. As Mrs. Goodyear read the stories, I looked at the pictures: big red dogs and monkeys on hard yellow covers. But today, I just wanted to go home. Maybe to play soccer, maybe to rest. I just wanted to go home.

Before the last class ended, we put on our shoes, jackets, and hats and took book bags, which had been left in the school hallway. I put on my clothes, smiling, because in my little life I had a great day. Usually, as students lined up for the bus, all the girls would blow kisses at me, blush, and put their heads on their shoulders. But that day was different; everyone was shying away, turning their bodies, curling their lips. I didn't know why everyone was behaving like this. Maybe because Mrs. Goodyear threw her shoe. The buzzer rang, and the students hopped on the bus.

I'd started my school adventures at the front of the bus, mouth closed, eyes and ears open. But as I got to know people, I made my way to the back, joking and screaming with others. Usually, smiles and dimples lasted until everyone got off; I was the last stop on the route, the last passenger.

But as this drive home started, everyone stared at me in a weird way, making conversations among themselves. With each student drop off, some students would say something to the bus driver; others would just exit.

Down to Heckman's Island and back, we drove past Garden Lots through the coastal little highway lined by the boulders of Blue Rocks. Once Blue Rocks was behind the bus, a church greeted me home into Stonehurst: the home of my heart, the place of my peace, the seat of my song.

The bus ended its route at a small hill; at the top of this hill was my home.

"See ya later," I said, confused by the looks on my peers' faces.

"Have a good evening, Adam", the bus driver responded. Her nostrils flared as she looked out at the boats resting on the tiny cove.

I leaped off the bus, the last step a huge height for someone of my age, the age of five. I looked at my house, and the door opened. A small Labradoodle (half Labrador, half poodle) busted out of the door and ran down the hill as fast as he could.

"Robbie," I yelled.

Robbie slid on the sandy road before he jumped on me. He usually licked my face and kissed me but that day was different. After a couple of kisses, he started to sniff and paw at my book bag. He'd never acted like this before. We walked up the hill and into my home. The house was green with white trim, a welcoming appearance. I opened the door; Robbie always went in before me.

"Hi, Bump, how was your day at school?" Mom said, embracing me with all she had. She smelled like processed fish and coarse salt when she came home from her job, unlike the smell of seaweed and rotten lobster traps that came from the shanties on the shortened shore. I don't know why she called me "Bump." Maybe because of a knock on the head I got when I was young, I should have asked. Mom just called me "Bump."

"All right," I said. "Just glad to be home."

"That's good. Do you have any homework?"

"No."

In primary, they never really gave you homework, but Mom was so intent on someday helping me with my schoolwork, she wanted the homework to start as soon as possible. I took my book bag off and gave it to my mother. She picked it up and cracked the zipper. With sudden disgust, her face coiled to the back of her head as she held my book bag as far away from her body as possible.

"What did you do at school today?" Mom's face in disbelief.

My mother took my book bag and showed me the inside. Just under my math book, to my surprise, was human feces. Smelly, stinky, brown human feces.

"Mom, someone pooped in my book bag."

Mom laughed, either because of the expression on my face or the explanation of the situation.

"Well, I guess I will have to clean it up."

Mom cleaned my books. I think she got me a new book bag. The school authorities believed they found who the "pooper" was, but that didn't stop me from going to Mrs. Goodyear's primary class. Today, I am more scared of a high-heel shoe than a piece of poop.

Stonehurst brought me lots of memories, but nothing more important than the time I cherished with someone special.

10. FISHING

In my younger days, I'd forgotten about the sea, for video games and the newest VHS movies captivated me. This was despite the fact that I woke up to the ocean every morning, the smell, the feel of the fog, the sunrise, its spirit.

It was the weekend. Dad was off the road, resting until the next time he would have to record his radio show, *Newfie 30*: jigs and reels, toe-tapping music from the province my namesake, Pelley, was from, Newfoundland. I was watching television when my father asked if I wanted to go for a row in the dory, to take a little trip on the water. Even though the sea was forgotten and memories fade, I didn't have the opportunity to spend much time with my dad, so I went to get some old clothes for the row on the sea. An old jacket, pants, and my rubber boots got me prepared. We took our jigs, a fishing tool that I easily learned to use aboard other voyages on the Atlantic.

As Dad rowed out of Robbie's cove, I put my hand in the water, similar to a fin giving direction to the dory. The water between my fingers gave me contentment in my heart. Dad rowed, the oars pushing the boat on the sunny, gentle sea, the white caps of the water turned into a polka-dot cloud day. We didn't get too far from the coast, just far enough so that I had to wear a lifejacket. Dad stopped to take a break. He wanted to know about school, new friends, my teacher, all that he missed from being on the road so much.

"Everything's great, Dad."

We hadn't talked long when I looked over the side of the boat and saw that there were schools upon schools of fish, so many fish, the water was hard to see. You could take fishing nets and pick up about ten mackerel. We were having fun, bonding with every fish that came off the hooks of our jigs, fishing lines wrapped around wooden frames. We had to throw some fish back. Despite all our fun, we had to go home. Dad was tired of rowing; the oars were heavy in the water.

I put my hand back in the water again, sore from the fishing line of the jig and the fight of the fish. That contentment now more in the heart, my being full of that satisfaction, fishing with my father.

We came home with so much fish, Mom didn't know what to do—freeze them or give them to the neighbors. I was a fussy kid, I didn't like mackerel. I went back to my video games, forgetting the sea again. The only thing that mattered was me and my dad. Although my parents were separated, those unforgettable moments, my family and the environment that surrounded me was so giving and loving, I never wanted to leave it.

11. HOME

I woke up and looked out of the window overlooking the cove where I would spend my childhood. The clouds looked like smoke bellowing from the horizon, getting breath from the sea and sky. It was an excellent day, judging from the serenity of the sky and the soundless sea that watched the smoke grow higher. I could smell the crisp air through the crack in the window. I was ready for today to be good.

I walked down the stairs. Mom was in the kitchen, where she spent pretty much most of her time. Pop was in his chair looking out the window, looking over his ship, which gave him his living, his life. *Evelyn* was her name.

Pop wasn't a blood relation. He brought up my mother when my real grandfather wasn't around, although my biological grandfather was a very respectable man. Pop couldn't read or write, but he was the smartest man I have ever known because what he knew—his work, his life, the sea—he loved and that was all he needed. Occasionally, he also needed a drink to take away the pain in his hands caused by the hauling of lobster traps and fishing nets.

"Hi, Bump," Mom said. She was washing some dishes that were dirty from snacks the night before.

"Hey, Mom, what are we doing today?"

"Well, after I get things cleaned up, we are going to take a trip into town."

"Can I get a toy?"

I always wanted something, wanted more. I never thought about the chest of toys I hardly ever played with, or the fact the main reason Mom was going to town was to put food on the table. As a kid all I thought about was myself. As an only child, if I wanted something, I usually got it.

"Sorry, honey, not today."

I started to fume, my fingers grasped my thumbs, my lips came tightly together, and my eyebrows almost dropped to the floor. I was mad. I started jumping up and down in a tantrum. I wanted a toy.

"Get mad all you want. I don't care. No toy today." Mom was saying you have enough toys to play with, and she had three mouths to feed, sometimes four. At eight, I couldn't comprehend that the hand that gave could only give so much. Mom continued to wash the dishes.

I immediately went to my room, stomped on my bed in ignorance, got my suitcase and packed a book, my teddy bear, a T-shirt, and some underwear. When I came down the stairs, Mom was at the door.

"Where are you going" she asked.

"I'm running away," I said, ready to open the door.

"Okay, see you later."

I was surprised by her answer, but that's what she said.

I opened the door and started down the hill. Before the door was shut, Robbie came chasing behind me and followed me down the hill. I reached the bottom of the hill and continued on a little further with my dog by my side. I stopped for a second and looked up the next big hill on that sandy road. Then I realized I was running away from everything—security, knowledge, wellness, love. All of this understanding arose in the mind of a child. I looked back at my home, and I knew it was just that.

"C'mon Robbie, let's go!"

I walked back up the hill and knocked on the door of my green and white house.

"Hello," Mom said, astonishment in her face as if she were looking at a stranger. Not many strange people came to the door in Stonehurst.

"Mom, I'm sorry. Can I come home?"

"Of course, you can."

Mom gave me a great big hug. We went to town. I didn't get a toy. I think Mom got Pop some rum. *Evelyn* didn't say a word.

Although our community was very small, I always went to a place to play a game I loved and found myself in a situation I didn't mind at all.

12. THE SEWER

On any clear day, any season, any time after noon, Stonehurst was a sports community. In the winter, we waited for the ice to get thick to play hockey, but we didn't play that often. In the summer, we played baseball and soccer in the small fields, but since there were so few kids, we didn't play that often. But every season—spring, summer, autumn, and in the winter— in the gymnasiums at school, we played basketball.

Only five of us were in the same age group. Aaron, the oldest, taught us how the sport was played and told us stories about playground victories that we all wanted to experience for ourselves. The Crofts were Doug and Dwayne. Doug was an architect of dump-truck cities, a grandparent's favorite grandson. Dwayne, the smallest package of energy I have ever seen, could throw a rock farther than a major league outfielder could. Aaron gave Dwayne the nickname Peanut; only he knew why. Al, a cousin of mine, wasn't interested in the sport we all grew to love in the community. His passion was working with his father and his tools in the family's red shed and skating at the local arena.

In the summer, many days it would just be Peanut and me, one on one, in the Crofts' driveway. We would ask Doug to play, but I think he was more interested in the newest high-tech video game. I too liked technology, but the game meant something to me. Sometimes Doug would come and sit out on the stoop of the small blue house and watch

Peanut and me play; sometimes he would take part. He didn't have a shooter's touch, just the occasional lucky roll on the rim.

I loved the game of basketball; it's all I wanted to do. The ball was my world, an escape into dreams—the fantasy of playing in front of thousands in arenas played out on dirt and gravel. Peanut and I played a lot of basketball. Many times, around supper, Aaron would drive toward home in his car, money and exhaust more important than a rubber Spaulding basketball. We would yell for him to come up. Seldom would he come, but he did once in a while. The older we got, our increasing responsibilities robbed the game from our heads but not from our hearts.

We played the heat out of the summer with hoops. We played basketball until all you could hear was your thirst at supper time. The only thing to drink was water from the hose at the side at the house. Doug would bring the ghetto blaster out on the stoop and play music. Peanut rocked to AC/DC.

Most of our games were like any other on the planet. One person would score, check the ball up top, another basket. But often the rubber basketball would take a bad bounce off of the rim, hit an awkward shaped rock and go right into a sewage drain that ran parallel to the Crofts' house. The longer the sewer ran, the larger the sewer became. The grotesque mix of urine and waste finally would run under a culvert beneath the sand sealed road and dumped into another small cove where fishing boats were hungry to catch their fish.

Many times, we knew how the ball would bounce so well, we could catch it before it went into the sewage. But sometimes, the ball hit the sewer with so much force it would be hard to retrieve it. We did have more than one basketball, but every one of them landed in the sewage. Peanut and I took turns retrieving the balls, usually depending on who missed the rim. We would straddle the sewage, one foot on each bank and pick the ball up with our fingertips. We would wipe the filthy, stinky, repulsive substances off the ball by rolling it through the grass next to the gravel driveway that was our court. We didn't care; our young lives were represented by that ball. Not even nasty, disgusting, vile waste could steal that gravel pick up glory from us. We watched for those brown spots every time the ball got in our hands, watching every dribble, and we continued to play with those shitty balls because they were all we had.

Those pickup games that brought us dreams of playing in arenas led me to a school team and a game at which I would meet someone for the first time.

13. RUN

I sat out in the hallway of Centre Consolidated School, by the snack shop, and waited. Some buses also waited there to pick up students and take people home after a busy day of classes. I was in Mr. Ruth's grade eight class. Mr. Ruth was a great science and industrial arts teacher. He was so skilled at building intricate things and a wise, straightforward educator; he was the carpenter at Centre. I should have showed him more respect than I did.

This day, my focus was not on the eye of the educator or the craft of the carpenter but on the game: basketball. All day, the ball ran through my mind. I wanted to feel the jersey on my shoulders. Anticipation filled me; excitement was in my hands. I waited in the hallway; some friends walked by, waited, and left. I didn't realize what I was waiting for until they arrived, the Warriors, the Hebbville Warriors.

In the tryouts for the "A" basketball team at Centre Consolidated School, it was difficult for students in grade eight to make the grade nine team. Centre Junior High went from grades seven to nine; the high school outside of Bridgewater, Parkview Education Centre, went from grades ten to twelve, amalgamating three junior highs—my Centre, Mahone Bay, and the school of the team I waited for, Hebbville.

With the sweat running down my face, I'd worked my ass off at the tryout, hustled for everything, basketballs, out of bound lines, exemplifying the defense that wins ball games. I made the team. Now, after playing several teams in the county, we were to play the best; we were to play the Warriors.

The team from Hebbville walked in with nice collared shirts and ties, appropriately groomed, as if walking into a business they knew so well that they owned it. Most of the Warriors were bigger than we were. They walked with confidence, chests out and chins up, ready to compete and accomplish all things they had practiced.

I didn't move from my seat. I tried to see tells, scout them, like a seasoned poker player learning the little things about his opponent. Or maybe I was just fascinated by the nature of this team as if I were going to play against the best poker player in the world. Anyway you look at it, I couldn't wait for the basketball game.

As the last Warrior came into the school, a giant for someone of my age, I sought out one of my best friends at that time. He lived just up the road beyond Blue Rocks.

"Hey, bro, they're here."

"What do they look like?'

Brent was my height but leaner, his pug nose twitched, and his curly hair was hidden by the way it was cut.

"They're really big, man."

"Think we can take 'em?"

"Hope so."

What the Centre Breakers basketball team lacked in God-given athletic ability they made up for with God-given heart and determination. The man that saw this will underneath our blue jerseys was our coach. Coach was not a perfectionist, he just wanted our true ability and best effort as much as our time allowed, in the classroom and on the hardwood court. He did not make a team from the people who threw the best behind-the-back pass or were the most popular in school; he picked a team that would listen, learn, and mature into not only a better basketball team but better students and people.

As Brent and I walked down to the locker room, we were joined by more of our teammates. Our color blue signified us as one. The only things that identified us were the numbers on our backs and the sneakers on our feet. I don't know if we bought the sneakers because they were in fashion or to generate speed. Either way, the more expensive the footwear, the more our feet felt like they had wings and no limits.

When we were all geared up for the game, Coach came in to motivate us. These were the Warriors, the best in the county. He didn't have much to say because I think he already knew that if we worked hard, focused, and used strategy determined by hours of practice, even smaller men could take down larger adversaries.

When Coach left the locker room, all our attention and anxiety about competition turned toward the captain, the best basketball player in the school. Samuel looked like a man who delivered pizza, an extra on any Hollywood film set. But the way he presented himself, he was a leader, the perfect captain for that day.

"All right, boys, this is going to be a tough one, but if we stick together, we can pull this one off. Put your hands in, Centre on three."

The boys and I positioned ourselves around Sam's hand, placed our own on top of his, and created a circle like the orange steel rim that represented our goals.

"One, two, three, Centre!"

We were ready. Jerseys on, laces tied, we lined up and waited for our warm-up music to start. The time had come. Basketball: the love of lonely life, the rant of running rhyme, the game of glorious gift. We ran around the court, which was filled with music coming from the speakers and the jubilation from our peers who stayed to watch us play on our home court. The gymnasium floor was starting to get old, from Christmas concerts and monthly dances, lunchtime activities and the game I love.

I was near the back of the line; all the eighth-graders were. I ran onto the court. The Hebbville team were wearing red uniforms, as if basketball was their blood. Their coach watched his team, arms in his pockets, his war machine prepared to tear apart another unsuspecting casualty.

We warmed up; we were ready. Sam went to greet the other captain at center court. The Hebbville captain, number five, was small, but his eyes showed all facets of the game, his eyelids putting out the fire not yet lit. The referees took their place, the blue and red stood around the center circle, the ball was tipped, and the game began.

From the tip, the game was controlled by number five. He summoned the ball, trained by relentless home practice, and he turned his efforts into a masterpiece of basketball art. He would pass by one, then fake out another; he would steal the ball like it was your birthday and he'd blown out the candles. There was nothing we could do; we might as well have given the ball to him and started to sing. Foul-line jump shots, three-point baskets with ease—he could play ball. Coach tried everything to stop number five: played zone, put together a different five players, even let Sam defend him. Nothing worked.

"Brent, you're in."

Brent went up to the scorer's desk and went in to the game. Usually, Brent got into the game before I did. It would make me jealous because I thought I was just as good a player as my friend was, sometimes better. But coach saw the game with a better eye than I did. Still despite all the players on the bench and the splinters in my behind, nothing changed. With number five's play and the support of the others on the Warriors bench, they had a comfortable lead going into halftime. We felt defeated; we could hardly feel our hearts.

We walked into the locker room with our chins on the top of our chests. Coach saw us looking as if the day were over.

"Boys, sit down." We sat and looked into our coach's face of knowledge,

"When is a game over at halftime? Never. Basketball is a game of runs. Their run was in the first half. There is another half to play. We now have twenty minutes to go on our own run. You look defeated. Why should we go out there right now and feel the game is over? Basketball is a game of runs. Let's go out there during this next twenty minutes, go on our own run, and win this basketball game."

We now had hope and a realization that this game wasn't over until we shook the other team's hand and when we all, both teams, heard the final buzzer. We were to go on our run. We were going to run them right out of our gymnasium. The second half started; I think I played for about two minutes. Still, no one could contain number five.

I noticed another player come off the Warrior bench. He was my height, with dark hair; among the players who were my age, I'd never seen anyone that young with a moustache. There was something about him, maybe his basketball finesse or that premature facial hair. Something. Like I knew him before I knew him.

The Warriors were still leading. We were lost; our coach called a time out.

"Boys, I think we've tried everything. Sam, now is your time. Take control of this game. It is your time to shine."

Sam knew what he had to do. He put on a basketball performance that would equal any piece of renaissance art or sculpture in a museum that human hand cannot touch. Only genius could have created this comeback. He made impossible fades like Bird; he passed with precision like Magic. The court was his; he would go coast to coast. Number five tried to defend Sam, but he would score. The Warriors would double team Sam, but Sam would pass and we would score. We crept closer and closer, but still, the Warriors would not let us take the lead.

With seconds left, we, the Centre Breakers, were down by one. The ball was in Sam's hands. He drove down the middle of the lane, spun to the hoop with number five guarding him, and shot.

Whistle. The referee's hand was raised; the other hand pointed at number five, sending Sam to the foul line to shoot two foul shots with no time remaining on the clock.

I sat on the bench, elbows on my thighs, and hands covering my sight. It seemed it was just Sam and me in that gym. It was quiet, even the Hebbville Warriors didn't cry much from their seats by their court. I couldn't look.

"Yahhh!" everyone yelled as Sam made his first shot to tie the game. I clenched both of my fists but didn't rise from my seat. One more. They had their run; we had ours. One more.

I once again put my hands over my eyes, hoping Sam would make what I thought was the easiest shot in basketball. One more.

"Yahhh!"

I looked up and saw Sam running straight for me, his hands in the air. I could see every tooth in his mouth. We won the game. We shook hands with the Warriors. I saw the coaches thank each other, as if they had enjoyed that game more than if one of the teams had blown the other out of the water. We all went back to Sam and patted him on the back—our leader. His skill and knowledge may have made him a great basketball player, but his presence, confidence and attitude made us follow him, and made Coach call him captain.

After accomplishments on the court, it was time for accomplishments in the classroom and achievements that were beyond expectations.

14. BLUE

The day was blue. No wind, no clouds. I didn't even realize how fantastic the sun made the trees smell; it was just blue, so blue. It was the day of my graduation from Centre Consolidated School. I was finishing grade nine, the place where my literal and social education had taken its course. First fight, first crush, first dance, first kiss. And now a ceremony with all the people with whom I'd shared those experiences.

I can't remember what I actually wore, but I know I wore a tie. Earlier I'd walked up the road to my mother's friend's house, a skipper of sail and song, so he could show me how to tie the knot. I still don't know how to tie a tie.

It was a day of academic achievement, honoring hard work in desks and homework in front of television. A couple of days prior we'd celebrated athletic achievement, honoring hard work in T-shirts and shorts and practice in front of nets and shitty balls. I didn't know what awards would be given to me, or what I thought I deserved. That night, I was named the most valuable player of the basketball team. I had been captain that year. We had a real good team but we lost to the Hebbville Warriors in county playoffs. The warrior with the moustache guarded me. It was a battle of inspired youth. Our own small rivalry.

When it came time to announce athlete of the year, my thoughts were of one of my peers, Mark. I always thought he was a better athlete than I was; his quiet demeanor followed his effort, his emotion was hidden by his performance. When Coach announced the person who earned the award, all I could think was Mark's name. Surprise tingled through my ears when Coach said, "This year's athlete of the year is Adam Pelley."

I have never had a bigger smile on my face since that moment. My cheeks were touching my hairline. Coach gave me the trophy. We both smiled for a picture.

A couple of days later, we were sitting in the gym for graduation, and all my loved ones were there. My mother and her boyfriend at that time, Tucker, a welder by trade who loved the sea, loved the wind in his face. The sea was him. And there was my dad, my grandmother, and my Uncle Fred, whose face should have been on every joker card in every deck of cards.

The graduation was a great ceremony. The principal greeted and thanked everyone; the student council president had her time. More awards were given. I was awarded another honor, the social studies award, by a great teacher, Mr. Smart. Social studies was always one of my favorite subjects. For some reason, I excelled at the topic; for that reason, on that day, I was given a medal. It looked like the insignia of the school, white and blue, with my name and acclaim on back.

More awards were given, and finally diplomas were handed out. The first set went to the people who had achieved their goals to get out of this school and on to the next one. A year's hard work and a couple pieces of paper gave them this opportunity. Then honors were given out by the vice principal; this year, they were designated by a new code. The Blue Society represented people who had grade averages of 85 percent to 89.9 percent. The Double Blue Society was for those with grades of 90 percent and over.

As the recipients of the Blue honor went to the stage, I was ready to receive mine. I didn't think my grades were significant enough to be the best, but they were substantial enough to obtain an honor. But the last person walked down the stairs, and I didn't become part of the Blue Society. The vice principal, Mr. Eddy, then announced the recipients of the Double Blue Society,

One recipient was a friend I'd played hockey with as a kid. He put me to shame on the ice, quick and smart; he listened. I'd always had a childhood crush on his sister. Before graduation, all the ninth-graders had gone to a camp on the outskirts of the county. It was a retreat to remember our days at school, and maybe a small warning on what was to come. My hockey and award-winning cohort played guitar with some classmates and Mr. Smart. They surprised me and made me stand up to sing, "Stand by Me." I sang halfway through, then sat down, truly embarrassed.

Another recipient was the girl with the big glasses and short hair who was always singled out and picked on, and today I regret that. One thing I don't regret is that she gave me competition in the classroom because sometimes I could not find motivation within myself. We would always try to find out who could get the better grade, the better mark, even sometimes the better comment from the teacher. She deserved all academic acclaim that came to her.

"Mark, please come up."

This was not a surprise; Mark was a better student than he was an athlete. Mark excelled at everything. If you asked him to build a ship in a beer bottle, he could probably do it before anyone else.

Watching those three accepting rewards for their tireless efforts, honors they could put on job and college resumes, I thought I had failed. I thought there was no way I had achieved this honor. Numb were my fingers and toes; sweat was on the top of my forehead.

"Adam Pelley, please come up."

Exhilaration, release.

I walked up to the stage, climbed the stairs, and shook the vice principal's hand. He gave me the Centre Consolidated School Double Blue Medallion. I saw many people smiling, especially my parents and my grandmother.

As the graduation ended, most of us went off to some event we'd heard about from friends and family. The day ending, everything was still blue, double blue now.

In the hall of the Centre Consolidated School, our four names are on the first of many plaques representing students' dedication and teachers' belief in their work. It was now time to meet new people, new teachers, and new opportunities. It was time to go to high school where my experiences would start to mold me into a man.

15. PANTHERS

It was my first day of high school. A new day, a new school, a new experience, a new beginning. A lot of my old classmates from Centre were still close to each other because it was all they knew coming into Parkview Education Centre, its own brave new world.

It seemed like the people I grew up with my whole life wanted to erase me from their minds with their unsharpened pencils they had bought for their first classes. Some would say hello; most would shy away. But maybe it was me who was that pencil, trying to make my mark on a place that would mold me; maybe I was the one who was erasing old friends.

The first day was the grade ten orientation day. All of us gathered in the cafeteria to see which homerooms we would be in for the next three years. For some reason, I sat next to the two tallest pupils in the student population. Scott left a school that he was supposed to grow into, coming to a place where he would have to gain respect all over again. He was a lone Viking from Bridgewater High School coming into the Panthers' den of about 850 hungry mouths. Tim was six foot eight and ready for whatever was to come; he was the best new basketball player to step foot on Parkview Panther ground, a former Hebbville Warrior, a giant. Then there was me, just me.

We heard our call. Coincidentally, Tim and I were in the same homeroom class with Mr. Johnson, the school's music teacher. I looked at my itinerary, my map of maturation into a scholar. I walked into the music room and sitting with his two bags was that Warrior, his moustache now grown into a goatee, his hair parted in the middle. With battles on the hard court, unknown glances in the Bridgewater Mall, and me being jealous because of the beauty of his girlfriend, I learned his name before we actually became friends, Jesse.

I sat near Jesse, actually beside Tim because I'd shared conversation with Tim earlier in the day. Mr. Johnson welcomed us to our new home. Most of us received his greeting, although there were always some students who didn't want to be there because they'd heard the same greeting the year before. This was our first day; the rest of the school would come back in the next couple of days.

At noon, people smoked in the parking lot, or ate in the cafeteria, or played music in Mr. Johnson's room, or played guitar in the hallways. But the temple of the lunch break at Parkview Education Centre was the gymnasium, where we played basketball. The gym was split in half by a border based on pickup tradition. At one end were the students who just played for fun, for comfort, for play. The other side were the players the whole gym watched. They loved the game and admired the spirit of competition. Usually, the older students would dominate the court and never leave it until it was time to resume class. Tim sometimes played on their team.

I'd always wanted to learn more about the game, so it seemed to me that even though my ability sometimes did not match up, my hustle would gain enough appreciation that they would let me play on the side of the court where the game was respected. I wasn't trying to put down the players who focused on fun, but the other side was where the game was played so well, people were entertained.

Over the next couple of weeks, I started to get to know everyone, and it seemed everyone knew me. Each morning, when I got to homeroom, Jesse would shake my hand, the way he did when the only thing we had in common were basketball sneakers and the heart for the sport.

Now, we were Panthers. As Panthers, we did many things together. We practiced basketball together, took tests at school together, and on the weekends, partied with friends together. I was comfortable with practice and school. I didn't know about the parties.

16. PARTY

The whistle blew and we would run, touch the closest line, and come back; run, touch the next line, and come back; run, touch the next line, and come back; run, touch the next line, and come back. Whoever finished the sprint—which sometimes made us sick—would have the dubious task of sinking two free throws. If the throws were made, practice was over; if they were missed, there was more running. After two more times of touching lines, Warrior number five, now a Panther, made both shots. Thank you, Ryan MacBride.

We all gathered at the foul line, and Coach told us about our upcoming games, so we could be prepared, aware of our potential, and presentable, wearing ties and nice shirts. Usually, the basketball team was comprised mostly of twelfth-graders. But this year, the team pretty much from the eleventh grade, except for the new guys: Tim, Scott, Jesse, and me. Sam was on the team too.

I usually got a ride with Sam into Lunenburg after practices; there, Mom would pick me up and take me home, but this night was my first look into what students say high school is all about. Instead of going home, I waited with Jesse outside the gym.

"When is your sister coming, Jesse?" I asked. My mind was not on basketball but on the night that was coming.

"She should be here soon."

"Hold on."

Just then, Boo came running out of the school, his bag hanging from his side. I can remember playing Boo in junior high basketball; he was a native of Mahone Bay. Even though he was older, it was his first year on the team.

Jesse's sister, Rebecca, drove a small brown Escort; the color matched the freckles on her nose, her big brown eyes, and her hair, which was tied in a pony tail. We got in the car and took off. Boo and Rebecca were very friendly, touching and having simple kisses. I didn't know they were together back then. The automobile finally brought us to Middlewood, the Edisons' home. I was a little nervous; there were not butterflies but a hummingbird in my stomach. I knew where Jesse lived before I was welcomed in; now, I would see the inside. We walked up the hill on a path made by trips to the store and to the bus stop. Jesse didn't say anything before I entered his home; I think he knew I would be a gentleman. We took off our jackets and shoes and walked into the living room,

"Dad, Mom, I would like you to meet Adam, the other grade-ten guard on the team this year."

Abe and Bette Edison smiled and welcomed me into their homes and lives.

"How you doin'?" both of them said to me, separately. "Nice to meet you." I could remember seeing Abe and Bette at every Warrior and Breaker game, clapping and cheering. To this day, I will say the Edisons are the kindest , friendliest, honest, most hard-working people I have ever met. Their work ethic also was apparent in Jesse's performance on the basketball floor. Before I took my shower, I met Buck, the Edisons' best friend. A black hound with a white belly, the only way he could greet me was with his slobber, which went all over my face and hands. I had to be extra clean for this night.

We got ready, all showered with cologne and perfume, each one wearing the appropriate attire for the occasion. Hopping in Rebecca's car, we started to drive, the destination was unknown only to me. We drove and drove further and further into the woods; the lights of the town were soon behind us, the only lights were the car headlights in front and the stars above us. They were a sign that where we were going was sure to happen, my first high-school party, my first glimpse of the "other side" of the educational social scene.

We kept driving and driving. I didn't think electricity existed this far back in the woods, where animals hunt their prey, and if you don't have a car your thumb becomes a ticket of transportation. One more back road and a driveway brought us to the house party.

We entered and found that it had already begun. People were smoking marijuana and drinking, Moosehead beer. Friends just having a few—to them, however, a few was about a case. As everyone mingled, including me with some new faces, no one could get away from the life of the party—someone I hadn't known long but already considered a friend.

Kirk Fisher was a comedian, but if something happened to one of his buddies, he was right there to back you up. Tall and lean, he was a risk taker, a man who would bend authority. If you ever needed a laugh, he was the one to go to; he'd probably make fun of our friend Clutz. If you needed a drink, Kirk would give you one. He was on the soccer team; he probably was the best all-around soccer player in the school. We were in the same math class. We did more laughing than linear equations. Kirk didn't like the color yellow.

As the party went on, the more intoxicating the rooms became. Almost everybody was drunk except for me. I may have taken a drink before, but I never had been drunk. I thought what the heck, let's have a drink. I had twenty dollars in my pocket, but it wasn't for me. Mom gave it to me for Sam, for all the trips after basketball practice to Lunenburg. I knew Sam didn't know Mom gave me the money for him. I started asking everyone if they had beer to sell.

"Do you have any beer to sell?"

"No."

"Do you have any beer to sell?"

"No."

"Do you have any beer to sell?"

"No."

I asked everyone; the answer was always the same. I didn't think I would ever get anything to drink, like everyone else had. Then some old friends who remembered me from Centre school tapped on my shoulder,

"Hey, bud, come with us."

We walked out of the house and up to a car. They opened the trunk, and there to my satisfaction was beer. Beer: the liquid of leisure, the drink of dance, the solution of sorrow. They had six beers. It was Maximum Ice. I had twenty bucks. We did the exchange. I went back in to the house and started my first beer. I think Kirk had ten down by that time. The beer was rasp and tough; my nose burned a little, but I kept drinking. There were many girls at the party. I wanted to talk to them, to see what they were like. I'd had short relationships at Centre, but nothing serious. It would have been nice to be near a lady for the night. The party went on; there was more drink, more smoke, kisses, even a fight, I think. I fell asleep on a chair, feeling cheery, way, way, way back in the woods where only certain animals God created should sleep.

17. THORN

We were at her place; her parents and siblings were gone for a weekend of relaxation and to build the relationship within their family. But she usually didn't go; she was older than her sisters, and this weekend was built for my visit, for us to be alone.

I met her at my first high-school dance. I arrived at the dance with Sam, his girlfriend, and another friend. Sam and I stood there in the same spot all night, knees locked and hands in pockets. When Sam's girlfriend wanted to dance, he would, but then he would return to his spot. The last dance of the night, she came up to me and asked the question I was too nervous to ask her. She had been dancing with her friends a few feet in front of me. I accepted the offer.

I found out her name, and I wanted to know more. Her dark eyes and dark hair invited me to find out more about her; but her dimples, lips, and the way she carried herself, made me weak. At first I couldn't even muster a hello in the school hallway, just a glance. As time went by, I had to get to know her. A tiny note with an offer from me led to a movie.

It was the end of the school year; whenever we had time to be together we would. We were like a simple equation. I was the question, so many different ideas in my mind on how to please and reach the answer that she represented. She knew what I wanted, what any sixteen-year-old wanted at that point in life. But she was perfect. She once said that I was perfect too, specifically the perfect height for her. So maybe we were neither the question or the answer but the equal sign itself, our minds, interests, and now hearts parallel. At that time in my life, whatever question or answer I came to, she was always there in my mind.

We spent the day at her house. She had a little drink, but I said no. We talked about a lot of things. Her starting university, what the summer would be like, could we still work everything out with her in university and me still in high school.

We ate; she had another drink; finally, we ended up in her room. We kissed and kissed some more; her lips were like penny candies and strawberry pie. She took off her shirt and shorts; I followed. We hugged and shared our warmth. I kissed her neck; her ears could hear my lips. I smelled and touched my way down her body to her panties. I slipped my two fingers underneath the lining,

"No," she said.

So I stopped. I smelled my way back up to her lips, ears, neck, my hand reaching down to her underwear,

"No," she said,

So I stopped. I sat up and thought there was something wrong with me, wrong with her, wrong with the moment.

I didn't think she felt comfortable with me sleeping in her room, so I went to sleep on the sofa in the living room. I felt awkward, that I'd disrespected her and the fact that she'd invited me over to her house for the weekend. I went to sleep, wondering if I would ever get to smell her again.

There was one bond that I knew I could always count on: my relationship with basketball.

18. THE FOUL

How I spent the summer between grades ten and eleven was up to me. My mother wanted me to get a job, to make a couple of dollars. I wanted to play basketball. Lunenburg is a small town, its history told by buildings, rum running, and the families that developed over generations. Every generation becomes different than the one before, even in Lunenburg. Some kids sold and did drugs, stole, and vandalized. But almost every kid, whether an honor student or a dropout who worked on the boats, came to the black asphalt court by the Lunenburg swimming pool to play basketball.

I'd wake up many mornings and at the break of dawn, my mom's boyfriend, Tucker, the captain of small ships and long liquor stories of the ocean, would put my bicycle on the back of his old, dark multicolored truck that I thought would never start. We would travel on the fog-laden road to town, and he would drop me off at the tennis courts, a two-minute cycle to that haven of black asphalt with white trim, the white painting the boundaries of the basketball court and a self-made foul line where I learned to make peace with patience.

It was another blue day, a day when there were no clouds. Everyone in town who played basketball knew each other from prior games, but in the early afternoon that day there were four of us playing ball while people watched from the pool.

Nathan, the captain of my basketball team at Parkview, was a quiet leader who sometimes screamed with enthusiasm, a comedian, a man who cared. Joel, Nathan's buddy, was a lunchtime basketball regular. If I ever had a problem, Joel would listen; he cared. Craig, an older teen from Lunenburg, played basketball once and awhile; he was a man who only cared for himself.

We started to play, two on two. I can't remember who was on my team, but I know Craig was guarding me. That day—under the blue, the sun, the small little audience now looking on from the pool—the ball was mine. Total control.

I took him left and hit a jump shot. I crossed over, leaving Craig behind me and had an easy layup. When the ball came in my hands, the ball went in the hoop. Craig was getting frustrated. I could see it in the wrinkle of his chin, in the grinding of his front teeth. I scored again; I finally had a grip on the game. With a jab step and a pump fake, I took him to the basket again. His feet now were cemented to the hot, black court; it seemed like I'd broken everything in his lower body—ankles, knees, even the tips of his toes.

I smiled; Craig was frustrated. I went back to the foul line and checked the ball. Craig's eyes started to turn bloodshot; his lips tightened. Before he gave the ball back to me, he hauled his fist back as far behind him as possible and hit me between the eyes. My vision filled with swinging stars, and blood poured from my nose into my hands. Nathan and Joel prepared themselves to see a fight, and Craig took a stance not only to start an altercation but to defend himself as well. With my hands over my face, I decided to do the one thing that I thought was appropriate, what a true lover of the game of basketball would do.

"Foul," I called, as I went and picked up the ball, blood all over me, and went to check it at the top of the key again. This made Craig even madder. He wanted to hit me again, but Nathan and Joel would not let it happen.

"Adam, go get cleaned up." Nathan said, concerned about the amount of blood I was spitting from my mouth.

"I'll keep playing," I said.

"You gotta get cleaned up."

I went to the washroom at the pool, cleaned my face, and stopped the blood that was coming out of everywhere except my ears. I went back out to the court. Craig was gone, but some new players, old friends, had arrived to play. I worked on my game all summer, went to camps, ran, did everything I could to prepare myself for the next season. I had to make that Parkview Panther team again. Without basketball I felt I was nothing, like that black asphalt court in the winter.

19. SPIN

Another year, another try out for the Parkview Panther basketball team. Before we put on our sweatbands and sneakers, we all figured it would be the same team as last year. Except for Scott, whose father had relocated to where his business needed him.

There was one spot free, and we all knew who would fill that spot. Simon, a former Hebbville Warrior who had watched Sam hit those free throws, came back from across the country where he lived with family. His tall stature and fancy footwork would be a perfect fit in Scott's absence. Strong. Sly. A Warrior turning into a Panther.

Although it seemed all positions had been filled, the tryout was intense, with sweat in our eyes and hardly any water-fountain breaks, defensive chants while we slapped our hands on the court doing stutter steps, passing with partners to see who had the proper technique. Then a scrimmage to see who could match up, who could play their number. Everyone was tired, hands gripping shorts at the knees, sweat from chins dropping to the floor.

Compared to all the students, I thought I flew. I thought I worked the hardest. I wanted to show that hustle outweighed slam dunks, heart meant more than athleticism. After the tryout was over, confident that I'd done the best job possible, I called my mother to see if she could come and pick me up.

"Hi, Mom," I said,

"Where are you?" she said with slurred speech. Whenever my mother has a little liquor, she changes and not for the better.

"Can you pick me up?" I knew the answer before I asked the question.

"Listen to me, you. Find your own way home. I'm never coming to get you at that damn basketball, you hear me?"

"How am I supposed to get home?"

"I don't care."

Mom was still trying to get over love lost. She and Tucker had split. Many nights she would sit on the kitchen counter and cry into her drink. I didn't know how to comfort her. I couldn't look her in the face without crying. I should have cried with her.

She hung up the phone. A great day had just gone awry. She was starting a new relationship with Ray but could not clear Tucker from her mind. I could see that Black Velvet whiskey in her hand. I put the receiver down, and my eyes started to fill. Ryan came over to see what was happening. I told him what happened with my mother. His girlfriend, Diana, came over and could see that I was not myself. The guy who always tried to make people laugh whichever way possible was not present; in his place was a distraught boy whose love of the game had torn him from the love of his family. The more my eyes filled, the more the tears ran down my face, my face was no longer full of sweat but the tears caused by a mother's scorn. As my eyes became wet and red, an assistant coach walked out of the office bathroom, and looked at me, cold. He didn't say a word to me. I didn't say a word to him.

Ryan invited me over to his place, a comfortable place, a place where I always felt at home. Ryan, Diana, and I rented some movies and went back to the MacBrides' house. Ryan reassured me there was nothing to worry about; he was sure I had made the team.

The sunrise was gold like an award waiting to happen. Diana picked us up, and we went to school. It was earlier than we went most days because it was the day some of our lives could change forever. Like I did every morning, I went to the gym to shoot hoops, kid with friends, and wait to hear that we'd have pretty much the same team we had last year. I had just made a three-pointer when I heard the voice:

"Pelley, you didn't make it!"

I looked at the door to see Tim; he was smiling but at the same time had a look of disbelief.

"You're joking?" I nervously turned to look at the entrance.

"I'm serious. You are not on the list."

I dropped the ball in my hands and headed straight for coach's classroom. Coach was also a history teacher. Every student I passed would look at my face and turn away, as if they knew. I turned the corner, and there, on the classroom door in front of me was the list. The whole team was the same except for three people: Simon, the one everyone thought would replace Scott. Seth, a tall tenth-grader out of Hebbville; a superb student who needed a lot of work on his game. And me, because I was not on the list. I saw Coach in his classroom, putting his lesson together on the chalk board. I stared at him; I wanted to know what I did wrong. He finally turned to me; his face showed sympathy and regret but also looked as if I'd done this to myself. I walked back up the hall to the cafeteria. Students lifted their eyes, then turned away, looked down, and frowned.

"You didn't make it either?"

I turned to see someone else who thought he was missing from the list as well. Zach, another tenth-grader, was more of a natural than Seth. But he lacked the scholastic achievement and obedience to authority that would not make his name appear on the Parkview basketball roster that year.

"This sucks!" I said.

We went to the cafeteria and considered our judgment: innocent in our dreams, guilty over what was real. I sat and watched Zach curse and swear about Coach. Then Jesse came into the cafeteria. Everything inside of him showed remorse; he looked at me and couldn't say a word. I couldn't say anything back.

"C'mon Pelley, let's go," Zach commanded. He gathered his belongings and walked out of the front entrance of Parkview. We walked down King Street toward Bridgewater; it was fifteen minutes with a good step. Zach complained about how much better at the game he was than Seth. He cursed Coach. I don't think I had heard so much foul language ever come out of someone's mouth in that short of time,

"What do you wanna do, Pelley?"

"Let's go get a donair."

The donair: the home of my hunger, the triumph of taste, the delicacy of my delight. We went in to the King of Donair on King Street and ordered our food. One donair, no onions, as always. As we waited for our lunches, I spun around in the plastic red seat.

"Pelley, wanna smoke?"

Zach pulled out a pack of cigarettes and gave me one. I'd never smoked a whole cigarette. I'd had puffs at parties and saw my mother smoke every day. But today, my name was not on that team list.

"Thanks, Zach."

Zach lit the cigarette, and I took a few puffs. I started to spin, spin, spin, like a top out of control, like a laundry machine spin cycle without a timer, inside the tornado never seeing the eye, just spinning while sitting. Spinning. As the spinning ceased, the donair brought me back. Not only did the cigarette make me spin, but my life was now spinning. What would life be like without basketball? They had a Division 2 team. I would be on the team; so would Zach.

From that day, my life changed. Basketball did not leave me, but reality dawned on me. Maybe the coaches wanted this year to be a learning lesson. But that year I learned more outside of school than I ever did in the classroom.

20. CLOUDS

"Meet me at my cottage at about 5:30," Joshua directed.

"All right. You got it?" I asked.

"You bet."

Two more classes, and I was on the bus home, thoughts of girls dancing, everyone happy, and before all this tiny night of glamour, sitting by the stove. I now lived on the Lahave River, near the yacht club. My mom's new boyfriend, Ray, took me in like I was his own. He was a man of his own opinions, very explicit at points, but always good to me. My respect is always given to the highest.

I washed up, put on some of my favorite clothes, footwear was not important—I'd be dancing. It was another high-school dance, but my friend and I wanted to try something different. Joshua was in my English class, skin and bones with sandy hair. If he had three shirts on his back, he would give you two because he knew he would still be able to keep warm. He loved the game of basketball like I did; he was a former Warrior, the biggest Boston Celtics fan I have ever met. A man of honor and substance, a friend who would never lead you to a trap.

I got ready, and Mom drove me up to Joshua's cottage. He was there waiting,

"Don't get into any trouble," Mom said.

"Yup," I replied.

I walked into the cottage on the river, straight to the stove, seats ready. We sat there and talked by the stove, interrupted by breaths of a clouded quiet peace. The more we sat by the stove, the more the peace grew. As we sat, stove hot, a car drove up into the driveway. We knew who they were.

Evan was a gentle person, a hard worker who held many jobs. Evan and Joshua had been friends before I met them, but now they accepted me as their friend. Evan got average grades, was somewhat popular, a nice guy. Evan and Joshua were on the volleyball team. But Evan was frustrated today.

I had known Lisa, Evan's girlfriend, since Mrs. Goodyear was throwing shoes. We never got along; we could hardly talk to each other. Her blonde hair and plump lips were very attractive, but her attitude always made me go in the other direction.

Lisa walked in the door and lost control.

"What are you doing, Joshua?" She didn't care about me.

"Sitting," Joshua said, "Do you wanna sit, Ev?"

"He is not doing that," Lisa proclaimed.

"All right, let's go," Evan said.

We all got in Evan's little gray car and headed to Parkview. The dance, the music, the lights, the stage, the girls, the new love. These were all the things I was looking forward to, and I think Joshua felt the same. But there was only one thing that could comfort me, my chair. I believe Joshua felt the same; he sat beside me. We'd sat around the stove a little too long; maybe the stove wanted us to come back. The girls would pass by, but I think they knew by our red eyes and our look into nothingness that we'd been around the stove too long. Some girls giggled, some shook their heads, but we enjoyed watching them dance.

The dance ended; once again, I failed to find a girl who wanted to sit by the stove with me or replace the stove itself. But my good buddy Joshua never had a problem seeing peace in the clouds when there maybe were no clouds at all. My friends made school a place where I felt accepted, even though I wasn't on the team. I watched some running competition in the Parkview gymnasium, a game I was certain I had the talent to play. But there was one team I knew I could not run with, a team that was beyond everyone in the province, maybe the country.

21. LIONS

The sky was gray with a muffled glow, like a lit candle on top of the clouds, warning the Parkview Panthers of the game that was coming. Although Parkview had many athletic banners, it could not match theirs. Although Parkview was on a little winning streak, it could not match theirs. Although Parkview had rivalry with a cross-town school, it could not match theirs. That night, it would be the Parkview Panthers versus the kings of Nova Scotia basketball that year, the kings of any court on which they stepped foot: the Queen Elizabeth High School Lions.

That year I played on the Division 2 team, but I attended all Division 1 games—to cheer, to motivate, to get underneath the skin of teams that entered the den. Sometimes I would dress up in a black panther costume and take attention away from the game with "off the wall" and "wing nut" antics.

I was talking to some of my friends when I saw the Lions walk in, led by their coach, a man who taught ethics through sport. He was truly their leader, directing and motivating his team to act as one. Knowledge overcame the individual; attitude became the team. The Lions came in like soldiers from beyond, more than just men, kings of this game, the jungle that we called basketball. It was soon time for me to take my seat; what I was sure to see was annihilation.

I sat by Jesse's parents. Abe loved basketball, had played as youth, and his child now encompassing his love. I enjoyed watching basketball with Abe.

During the warm-up, you could tell all the boys were intimidated from the way they were looking at the Lions. The only one with confidence was Ryan. He could go one on one with Michael Jordan and be intent on winning.

The game started, and the Lions ran like the Lahave River that was across from the school. They didn't stop; they ran fast breaks with tip passes, low post moves so fast Simon almost lost his shorts. It rained three-pointers, as if they were putting coins in a wishing well. Their wish was for some team in the province to give them competition, to give them a game.

I remember the Lions because of their performance on the court. Their shooting guard was a ball-handling wizard with a slick jumper. Their center was a rebounding machine. One forward was hustle, heart, and heat on the defensive end. The other smoother than satin, with a shooting stroke made for the arc. Then there was the pilot, the lion tamer, the captain. With Lion's coach giving orders, it was his game to carry. Lightning could not compare to his quickness, seconds were too long; he was so fast he could catch the bullet before it left the chamber. He was meant for the game; the ball was meant for him. With his height, stature, and handling of the ball, he was the best guard I have ever seen play at Parkview.

At halftime, Queen Elizabeth was winning. Points didn't matter; I was in awe.

The second half was the same; the Lions were synchronized, the Panthers followed their lead. As the points increased for the Lions, the benches started to play. Jesse always got in the game, but he got a little more time this game, making Abe even happier. At the end of the game, the gym was still packed to capacity. No one could tame the Lions. No one cared about the score. They won, and the Lions were kings.

I was leaving school one day, going into town to meet some friends, asking if anyone could give me a short ride.

"Pelley, get in the car," my former Panther coach said.

"Thanks." We left the parking lot in his beat-up car, and it was as if I was about to see next year's list on his classroom wall,

"Adam, I don't think you will be on the team next year. Some of us have come to a conclusion. We don't think you have a future in this sport. You won't play at the university level; you might sit on some bench at a small college. You will never play in the NBA. Do other things, but I don't think basketball will be in your future at Parkview."

I didn't say anything, just stared at the Rolling Stones CD case that was between us. He dropped me off; I thanked him. It was at that moment I decided to move to Halifax to live with my father. I took a cigarette pack out of my jacket and lit a smoke.

22. IRISH

"Pelley, tell them about what they're gonna walk into," said my new basketball coach.

I had moved to Halifax to live with my father and his new wife. I played basketball all summer. Now by charm, wit, and lots of pleading I was Irish, Saint Patrick's Fighting Irish, the Lions High School adversary.

"Is this Bridgewater?" Michael said, as we came upon the lights of the town. Michael was the epitome of Irish basketball; small in stature, huge in every other aspect of the game.

"Boys, this place will be so packed, it will be hard to inbound the ball. It's gonna be loud, the juices are gonna be flowin'." I was coming home to where I used to play pick up and be a Panther. This night was Parkview versus the Fighting Irish. I didn't know how I would be received: garbage thrown at me or a standing ovation. I hoped neither. Lunenburg County is basketball country, culminating at the pinnacle of boyhood dreams. Every young child wanted to play at Parkview.

I navigated my team to the school. My teammates were not ready for people to be at a game an hour in advance; usually they were there to attend the girls' games. The boys from Halifax were all looking forward to this game.

When I got through the doors, I headed straight for a telephone to call Mom,

"Hello."

"Hey, Mom."

"Hi, hon, are you at the school?"

"Yup, are you coming?"

"I'll try my best."

"C'mon, Mom, you have gotta be here for this."

"I'll be up."

My new coach, the coach of the Irish, knew the game well; it was like he had the luck and he used it with precision. I went to Saint Patrick's because I thought I would fit in; there were spaces to fill on the team. I also played football that year. I had been in the hallway at the beginning of the year and one of the captains approached me and asked me to come to practice. I played fullback. One game I had seven carries for 140 yards. Nice.

We all got dressed; we had to win. All the players were pumped for this game because they knew it meant a lot to me. Coach gave us our pep talk. We were ready to fight.

We came out on the hardwood floor—Parkview's emblem and panther painted in the middle—for shoot around, and the stands were already packed, but no Mother. I knew she would come. I kept doing layups, thinking about her. Every time I met a Panther at half court, a friend, I shook his hand. I shot one more time and saw Mom sitting by the Edisons, uncomfortable and awkward. I went over and kissed her on the cheek, to show her everything was all right.

We were in the den. I thought since I was on my old home court, I might get the privilege of starting the game, but I didn't. It looked like some of the crowd was disappointed. There was a new coach for the Division 1 team that year, the man who coached me alongside Zach on the Division 2 team. I believe he was behind the decision to keep me off the list, a decision that helped make me Irish.

We got off to a great start, but the Panthers wouldn't let their prey get too far away, "All right Pelley, let's go," Coach said. I had been ready for this since that drive in that beat-up car. Sitting by the scorer's table,

I could hear the crowd talking. The whistle blew, I was in the game. An appreciative, appropriate, applause followed. Jesse was on the floor, but we did not guard each other, a sign of respect. Jesse was captain of the team that year, which was well deserved.

I was on the floor for about thirty seconds when I stole the ball from one of the guards and had a breakaway layup. I couldn't mess this one up. I went to put it in the hoop but it bounced right off the glass and over my head. The whole county laughed. I laughed too.

The next time down the floor, I had to redeem myself; I'd just shot the biggest brick of my life. The ball came in my hands and I took it straight to the hoop with all the pride I had ever learned in the game. I got the call. Two shots. It was the first time I'd been at the line in the Parkview Gymnasium with any jersey other than one with a panther on it. It was the first time I heard my name chanted, like they knew my free throw, the easiest shot in the game, in the walls of the Panther den.

I made one of the two.

The game continued, we had the luck of the calls. The game was flowing right for us that night. Most people in the game knew me for my shot, quick but not for any guaranteed accuracy. I was accurate enough to defend; respect that before the drive. The boys passed the ball, swung it around, and there I was open, behind the three-point line. I shot, and it went swift through the hoop, making the sound all players love. People cheered. Kirk pointed at me, Joshua stood up and clapped, Jesse had a smile on his face.

It was a hard-fought game, the Irish prevailed, the people of the county were not as disappointed with this game as they had been with others. We all shook hands. It was the first basketball game my mother had seen me play since elementary school. After that night, we each had our rivalries, cross-town clashes; we played games where the competition took us. The Irish and the Panthers came to the same fork in the road, where one was left and one proceeded.

The Dartmouth Spartans were the hosts for the regional playoffs that year due to their winning season and the way they handled the game. There was one more team to qualify, as the Spartans already had. By chance, Irish luck, or the wish to regain respect, it was the Saint Patrick's Fighting Irish versus the Parkview Panthers. The game would determine which team would advance to the provincial championship tournament.

The small gym with its hard, slippery floor was cold, but there was heat, generated by the hope of continuing the season, the thought that this last game for one team would mean a couple more games for the other. Jesse's parents were there; I knew he wanted this more than anything. He had never tasted provincials; neither had I. This would be a ride.

It was close from the beginning, but we went on a run and they couldn't catch up. We started running fast breaks with a steady pulse; I finished them with tip passes. The ball was going in the hoop. The Irish were going to the provincials. I can't remember the final score, but we won by seven or eight points. And I scored seven or eight points.

Shaking hands at the end of the game, everyone looked at me with decency. Then Jesse, tears in eyes, his high-school basketball career over, hugged me. It felt like I'd done something bad to my friend, but I couldn't apologize.

"Good job," my former Parkview coach said.

"Thanks," I replied, happy.

I went over to see the Edisons, to see how they felt,

"You did it," Abe said. Did what? Got back at the coach, made it to provincials, proved I had a small place in this sport. I wish I could have shared the tournament with Jesse.

We lost in the first round of the provincials in Riverview, Cape Breton. That year's champions were the Dartmouth Spartans, the team whose home gym had hosted the final competitive basketball game: Jesse versus me, the Panthers versus the Irish. We started off as rivals, became friends on a team, and finally as rivals once more showed mutual respect for each other and the game we loved.

Basketball had been my love since childhood, but the clouds I'd shared with my friends started to guide me in another direction. Darkness started to grow. The only thing that could penetrate its blackness was the love I had for the ball.

23. MARY JANE

I returned to Parkview for my fourth year of high school. My tenure at Saint Patrick's was cut short due to school books that were never opened and smoking a little too much. I was staying at the Fishers' home for a while; they took me in like I was their own. Mom and Ray had taken the Winnebago to Florida for the winter.

Kirk and I were waiting for Smoky and Jesse. It was a gorgeous day; the sigh of the sky leaped into the trees and grass, into our lungs, our eyes. Jesse was going to Lunenburg High School to upgrade his credits for acceptance into university. Smoky would drive him in his little gray Ford hot box. Smoky had grown up with Jesse and Kirk and had been a friend of mine for four years. With his short, black hair and a stubborn nose, he would take advantage of any situation he could, like a pirate in the fog, lurking. Whenever you saw him he was smoking—in his car, by the school, in his house. If he was some place where he couldn't smoke, it was clear he couldn't wait to light up.

Smoky picked us up, and we drove toward Parkview. I went back to school to get my diploma and to try to get to those institutions where no one can afford to buy the books. However, the social education of high school became more important for Smoky and Kirk. We got to the front doors of the school, and the vice principal was standing there. I felt a jolt in my soul, thinking that we were in trouble for some forgotten action.

"How you doing boys? No school today, they are tarring the roof. Make sure you are here tomorrow. On time!"

We all said thank you, then, coasting down the driveway, we celebrated. A whole day with nothing to do except smoke. Mary Jane: the beast with beauty, the silence with storm, the calm with calamity. We put our plans together, but none of us had any money. We still had to go to Lunenburg to take Jesse to school, but since we had the day off, he wanted to enjoy it all, too. We got to Lunenburg and looked for Mary Jane, but nothing; maybe it would be a day without her.

A glimpse of the Irish, a pot of gold, crossed my mind. To get my grades from my year in Halifax, my mother had to pay for a biology book I had lost. The teachers at Saint Pat's said if I ever found the book, they would reimburse my mother.

"Do you wanna go to Halifax, Smoky?" I asked, thinking this plan might work.

"Why?" Kirk asked.

I told them about the biology book. I had been issued the exact same edition for my class that year at school. We would go to Halifax, get reimbursed for the biology book, then have some money to spend time with Mary Jane. Jesse and Smoky thought I was crazy, but Kirk loved Mary Jane.

"If you're not going to drive to the city, then I'm hitchhiking," I said.

"I'll go with ya," Kirk said.

This was Kirk's introduction to the road; hitchhiking was a gamble. But Kirk loved to take chances. He loved a card game more than he loved math tests. He loved Mary Jane most of all.

"Can you drive us as far as the highway, Smoky?"

I know he wanted to say no based on the sour look on his face, but he did. There were about 120 kilometers between Halifax and Bridgewater. I used to hitchhike from Bridgewater to Halifax all the time; my love for Mary Jane encouraged me to make the trip every Friday, so I could share her with friends. The red haze that she created in my eyes made me think of her more than I did basketball; her smell was an inescapable part of my youth. I can remember the last day I was to hitchhike with her, after my last exam, but Joshua came and picked me up.

Kirk and I started our hike on exit 11 at Blockhouse. It wasn't long before we got picked up, and a few conversations with pleasant strangers and a thank you later, we were at Saint Pat's. Kirk waited outside, while I went in, barked, begged, and lied to try to get the money for that biology book. The principal knew my mother had paid for the school book, so she wanted to give me a check. I told her I needed some money for gas. My car was running on empty. If they gave me all the money, they knew where it would go. Anywhere but Mom. The teachers of St Pat's knew of my deal with Mary Jane. In classes she would fill my lungs, stain my eyes.

So with a fifty-five dollar check and the fifteen dollars they gave us for gas, neither of us were going home without a taste of Mary,

"Who can we get to cash this check?" Kirk asked; he would do anything to get this money,

"What about your Dad?"

"No, don't wanna do that!"

"Evan!" Kirk pointed at me. Evan had started going to school at Saint Mary's University, also known as SMU, in Halifax. We walked down to the university, not in a rush, but fast enough to put a little perspiration in our shirts. We knew where Evan's dorm was; he had invited us there to party before. He could probably get the check cashed and introduce us to Mary Jane.

From Evan's room in the high-rise Loyola student residence, you could see the whole campus: The Tower, where athletics were key; the Student Union Building, where student politics were the lock; and gray buildings for learning, where study was the door. The green turf in the center of the school was where many battles of the Husky (team name) competitive hunt took place.

We walked into his room. Evan had a smile on his face like he had been out all night and was still partying. He invited us in to sit down.

"Can you do this for us?" We were desperate, desperate for Mary Jane in our lazy minds.

He said he could find Mary Jane for us, but could not cash the check.

"You could try Simon," Evan suggested.

This Simon was a different Simon than the one who played basketball for the Panthers. This was a different high-school classmate, another Panther. He was a great athlete. We went to Simon's room. He was there. I forged my mother's name on the back of the check. He cashed it. I thanked him.

Mary Jane can open your eyes so far you become blind, cover your mind so that you cannot see, show that everything burns into nothing. She can make stars and the universe reachable, bring peace with the pleasure she creates. We went back to Evan's room and headed over to the railroad tracks behind the university. It was us and Mary. I smoked. It was starting to get late, and Kirk and I had to hitchhike back home. We thanked Evan and took the city bus out to the highway. We had one more conversation with Mary Jane.

A van picked us up, a prop guy for a television show called *Black Harbor*. He dropped us off around Chester. We got picked up again and drove almost all the way the way to the Fishers.

We'd gone to Halifax with nothing, just a school book. We came home with nothing, just a little piece of Mary Jane for Kirk's brother. We cheated the road, cheated our friend, and even ourselves. Once we were back at school, could we cheat the game?

24. CARDS

A couple of things were inevitable at Parkview Education Centre: classes, smoking off property, clams and chips on Friday, basketball at noon, and cards in the cafeteria, particularly a game called whist. The rules were simple: four players with partners; people bid; eight won hands were a book; players bid over the book, one to seven—seven being a perfect hand or what is called Boston. If you had a three bid, then you and your partner needed to get eleven hands. Whoever won bid called trump, suit, high card, or low card. You won when twelve hands were won.

During my last year at Parkview, if I had to find Kirk he would be either smoking or playing whist. Education wasn't for him; he had no interest in it. When I was in class, I always raised my hand. When I was younger, I would answer the questions. Now the teachers knew what I was going to say before I said it. Sometimes they just said "go there" before I even asked, "May I use the bathroom?" They couldn't say no; all they would say was "just don't be too long."

I hardly ever went to the washroom; instead, I headed straight down to the cafeteria to play cards. Whist becomes very easy if you can wet your fingers on it. I walked in, and of course, Kirk was playing with some other people.

"I'm in," I said.

We reached a point where the question was not who was the better player but who was the better cheater. Sometimes, we would bid

"Boston" and win. When Kirk and I faced each other as a team, people always wondered how we got the good cards. Only the people we joked with a lot would accuse us of cheating. Cheating was all in how the cards were dealt.

We had a free period. Kirk and I were dominating another game of cards. I saw Smoky walk in. I had a little money, and I believe he knew it,

"Wanna go to Crousetown?" Smoky asked.

"Yup," I said, both of us nodding to Kirk to come along.

We jumped in the little gray hot box and did the drive Smoky could do with a blindfold on. About a twenty-minute drive out of town was where Mary Jane lived, Crousetown. The drive there was always a bit tense. I knew what the outside of Mary Jane's house looked like, but not the inside.

Kirk and I stayed in the driveway, and Smoky went inside. I never knew if someone was going to come out with shotguns or baseball bats, or set some crazy dogs on us. Kirk was a little nervous as well. The more time passed, the shorter my breath became, my heart a little limp. Kirk wasn't talking much; he was worried Mary Jane wasn't there. It was on my mind too.

But as always, like a superhero, Smoky came out of the door with a big smile on his face. Mary Jane was getting out of the house, she was coming with us.

Smoky left the driveway and drove towards Hebbville, to the old railway tracks, where the rails were removed, and parked. I smoked. Mary Jane looked good; her face was like a cloud that brings sound on storm-filled days. The experience was like sitting by an ordinary stove with a friend.

We could have had some more, but we wanted to get back to Parkview for lunch—not for the clams and chips but for noontime basketball. I had a cigarette, and we got to school just in time. We were one of the first teams on the floor and we wanted to stay,

"All right, boys, you know what to do."

"Crousetown zone" as all of us slapped the floor and started to play our own inspired special defensive scheme. Clutz was always on our team. He was not very athletic, but he was a good friend and tried hard so we picked him. The fifth spot was for who ever wanted to play the zone, whoever wanted to play the game.

The zone worked a lot. Get a rebound, give the ball to Smoky, tell him to go. Hoop to hoop, back to the Crousetown zone. Kirk would hit an easy jumper. I would pass the ball off to Smoky or Kirk, an easy two. Clutz would lose the ball out of bounds; he tried. But it would usually be Clutz to hit the winning shot. I would pass the ball, create the open shot, take advantage of the extra hand that everyone in the gym knew we had, Mary Jane.

25. DEED

I made it; I was a university-bound student. Acquaintances might have said it was unbelievable; friends would have said, "Adam, we knew you would do it. Unbelievable!"

My apartment was a rundown building at the end of Dutch Village Road, a half-hour bus ride to the school that accepted me, Saint Mary's. I was in town earlier than other friends who were moving in for school, so I contacted some old buddies from Saint Pat's. Bill decided to come over and see the new pad, which was perfect for a single bachelor entering the life of indulgence. Bill was probably the only person I'd been honest with at Saint Pat's. I told everyone else I was from Bridgewater, which was my place of learning but not where I slept, so I lied. I was with Mary Jane for almost every class, so I lied about my education, my ability in front of my teachers. I lied to people who laughed and called me friend. I hope the people I laughed with the most remembered me for the good times on the field, in the school hallway, and my South Shore accent that has never left me.

We decided to get a movie and pick up Mary Jane. We went to Blockbuster and searched for a while to determine what our entertainment would be. The answer was *Boogie Nights*, a movie about how adult entertainment can create big dreams and small fortunes but ultimately still ruin lives. We got back into Bill's big red van and headed out to pick up Mary Jane, an easier pickup than the movie we had selected. The movie made me think of younger days, of times alone.

In the green house in the community of Stonehurst, where I grew up, there were two cupboards: a larger one at the bottom for storing big things like cereal and flour and one that was higher up; I could just reach the handle. Whenever I opened that top cupboard, I noticed videotapes on the top shelf. For years I wondered what was on those videos—cartoons, news stories, *Hee Haw*? One day, after school, Mom went to town to do some grocery shopping, and Pop was off with *Evelyn*. I had to find out what was on those tapes. I took a chair, stood on it and retrieved a tape. The tape was black; there was no label. I decided to watch it.

The tape was pornography. Men and women having sex. I was getting to the age where I was starting to think about girls in a different way, like I wanted something from them, particularly certain girls at school. Watching more and more, my wonder started to dwell on the deed. The more I watched, the more the deed was done. The lonely deed has no virtue, no care, only a secret hidden past where regret could not fathom my woe. I missed some of my childhood because of these black tapes. They became an addiction. I'd be invited to go sailing on a perfect afternoon, to go for supper with family, play basketball with Peanut, but I would stay home and do the deed. I think girls were not attracted to me because somehow they knew I did the deed (or they were intimidated by the amount of hair on my body in high school). It was darkness in its infancy. I did the deed before the deed could be finished, I cannot remember the last time the deed was done.

Bill and I got to the apartment and sat with Mary Jane. I smoked. It was the first time her haze had been spread throughout my own place. We tried to put *Boogie Nights* in the videocassette recorder but it didn't work. We tried rewiring, changing outlets for the power plugs, reconfiguring the TV stations—nothing. That night, there would be no movie, just Mary Jane. I never took the movie back, I think Jesse has it. On that night, September 2, 1998, Swiss Air flight 111, departing JFK airport in New York on its way to Cointrin International Airport in Geneva, Switzerland, crashed into the waters off of Peggy's Cove and Bayswater, Nova Scotia. All 229 people perished. Engraved stone memorials were erected later at Peggy's Cove and Bayswater.

After the tragedy off the shores of Nova Scotia, many people looked for a light to embrace, something to let them know there is hope in the face of fear and loss. But when it came to me, despite the darkness in my life, the tapes, and the sweet smoke that filled my body, hope was the last thing I was looking for.

26. VISION

It was frosh week, classes had just started, the girls were wearing their best clothes, the library would be empty. One night there was a concert at the Tower, showcasing talents I'd listened to regularly since I was a child: Tone Loc, Rob Bass, and Maestro Fresh Wes. I waited for Jesse to come out of his last class because we had a date with Mary Jane by the railroad tracks. We were on time for the date. All we needed now was some beer to fill our bellies. That was not night a night for sorrow, it was a time to sing and dance.

We were in a line to get into the Tower. Everyone was restless, irritated that it hadn't opened on time. I walked up to the security guard at the door.

"Are you gonna let us in?"

"We can't yet, they're fixing something."

"Bud, our ticket says you are supposed to let us in," I said, with a little hostility in my voice.

"There's nothing I can do."

"If you don't let the students in, in about five minutes, you're gonna be responsible for what is gonna happen!"

I left and walked back to the line near Jesse; a lot of our buddies from home started to join us. As soon as I got into line, the door opened, and we were allowed in. I started buying drinks, for myself and for the others. My first drink was rye and ginger. It started a blinding good time.

There were people break dancing, friends toasting each other, liquor and more liquor. I believe that is how you are introduced to university life because if you live on campus it is hard to escape it. If you can get the total "university" experience and receive a diploma with honors, peace and respect be with you. We had our own table; some more friends from Bridgewater had driven in for the show. These rap artists had meant a lot to them growing up. We started drinking. After more beer and fantasies of being with the girls who smelled like cherry cheesecakes, the stage was set, and we drank more.

Maestro came out and rocked the place. About a thousand people were enjoying the performance. Peanut used to play the Maestro's "Black Tie Affair" tape on the ghetto blaster while we shot hoops and cleaned crap off basketballs. We drank even more.

Rob Bass and Tone Loc got up on stage and may have started the beginning of my new life,

"Does anyone freestyle?" Tone Loc asked

All my friends started chanting, "Pelley, Pelley, Pelley."

The guys on stage picked some other guys first, but they picked me last. The boys cheered. I was so drunk I could hardly stand. I got up on stage looking out at the new freshman class, my friends, and the liquor booths at the back of the Tower. The first guy couldn't rhyme "me" with "be." The second guy rhymed "Ice Ice Baby." The third guy sounded like he shouted out something respectable but not a freestyle. Then it was my turn.

"What's your name?" Tone Loc asked.

"Pelley," I responded, getting my balance on one foot.

"What's your name?" Tone Loc asked again.

"Pelley," I yelled into the microphone.

"All right, Pelley, let's see what you got."

I told the DJ to slow the beat a bit; I was so drunk I could remember only the first two lines of my rap:

"Well, this is my first year at SMU,

I'm so drunk, I know you are too."

The place erupted; I kept free styling. Before that, I used to freestyle only at parties with my buddies, drunk. That night was magnificent; dreams sometimes come true, although they might be a little cold and funky.

A girl came up to me, but for some staggering reason, I ran away. She was pretty, not enough to be in a pageant, but pretty. When she came near, I ran; maybe it was the liquor running. The rest of the night I kept running, in particular to the liquor booths until they said no more booze. I was drunker than drunk could drink is drunk. I took a cab home, capturing the night in my mind. I went to bed, thinking about classes the next day.

I woke up, still buzzed from the night before—the booze, the people, the stage. I went to sleep free styling; I woke up free styling. My mind could not stop rhyming.

I got to school, and everyone looked at me; they were giddy. "Awesome rapping," one girl said, as she passed by me in the quad. "That was awesome," somebody else said before I could thank the first girl. In class, I'd turn my head and catch people looking and then turning away, hoping they wouldn't make me notice.

"Good job last night."

"Great rapping."

It seemed like everyone knew me, and I didn't know any of them. After classes, I had to find someone who was a friend, someone who knew me. I walked the two blocks to Joshua's apartment, apartment 808. He worked nights at the Superstore on Barrington Street, but it didn't bother him that much when I knocked on the door.

"You missed it, man," I said.

"Missed what?"

"The concert. They got me free styling on stage."

Joshua and I used to listen to Tone Loc and Rob Bass as we were driving around Bridgewater, looking for a game of basketball or so bored there was nothing else to do. Mary Jane jumped in the car once in a while.

"Dude, go home, get cleaned up and we will meet up with Evan later on. Neither of us has to work at the store tomorrow." Evan worked with Joshua at Superstore too.

I was on the first bus to my apartment, cleaned, on the first bus back down to South Park Street; then I took the short walk to Joshua's apartment building. I knocked on Joshua's door, and he was ready to go. We headed to Evan's apartment on Inglis Street, the place where revelation, truth, and the beginning started.

"What's up," we both said separately, shaking Evan's hand.

"Do you guys wanna go for a walk?"

Evan was seeing a young girl named Heather, a girl who had everything, and she knew it. Her view was right; everyone else had to see her way. We walked into Heather's house. It had an inconceivably stunning interior, an immaculate smell; it was a house into which it was an honor to step. Evan took us through the mansion, showing us astonishing artwork and several investment plaques that Heather's father had made. Some for millions; some for millions more. Joshua and I looked at each other to see if we could get into a business like this. Overwhelmed by the amount of money that man had controlled in his hands, we left, thanking Heather's parents for letting us into their home.

"Time to take it," one of my friends said.

They gave me some magic mushrooms, chocolate flavored; I didn't hesitate, I opened the bag and poured the magic into my mouth. We went back to Evan's apartment, and Mary Jane was waiting on the table next to the television. There was a futon in the middle of the bachelor pad, and a small lazy boy beside it. I quickly sat beside Mary Jane in a kitchen chair by the table. We sat down and I smoked. There was the privilege of the bong that night, and I would clear the smoke every time I used it.

There was a knock at the door, and a kid named Kris entered. He was one of Heather's friends. I introduced myself and Mary Jane. He gladly accepted. We sat around and played Tekken, a combat video game and made some peace with Mary. It was my turn to take the bong. I threw all of the smoke back into my insides, and a simple thought of Oak Island went through my mind,

The light.

Instant eternity.

A blank page.

I awoke, sitting on the futon, not on the chair where the thought of the island that brought me the vision of God or the vision of my own soul. In the light, was a chest, open, but I could not make out what it was.

"Pelley, you all right?" Joshua asked.

"Yeah, a little cold."

"Should we call an ambulance"

"No, I gotta write a book,"

"You what?" Evan said, confused.

"I have to write a book about Oak Island."

"It's already been done, it's called *Treasure Island*," Kris responded, thinking he had all the answers.

"No, I gotta write a book about Oak Island."

I had to write something about the place I believed was the final resting place of the chalice of Christ or about how that chalice rests within us all. I had to write about the search for the ultimate pirate treasure, that cup, which leads to many lives being lost at the end of a noose or, in modern times, by mechanical means. I had to write about vision. The vision I saw when I was the love my parents shared at their wedding. The light that is within us all. The mystery that is Oak Island. The mystery that is love.

They all looked at me with confusion, not understanding what they were seeing, maybe a little fear.

"I think you need to sleep, Pelley. Come sleep on my couch at my place." Joshua was a friend being a friend in a time of need. Joshua and I walked back to his place. I struggled a little, trying to realize what had just happened. What I saw was good.

"Good rapping last night," a girl said as she walked by with a friend. They looked back, laughing.

"Thanks," is all I could mutter.

We got back to Joshua's, and I wrote something on a small piece of paper, something that would define the night. I gave it to Joshua. Joshua said he threw it out. That night I did sleep, but that was the night my life changed.

27. LOVE

After that all-seeing night, birds sang higher, the air felt better in my nose. Dogs looked at me differently, not with love but wonder. I felt like I could grab the sky because it was mine. But the clouds belonged to someone else.

When I first returned to school after my most high learning experience, it was like I would write the answers in class with notes before we got the test. I am not saying I answered every test perfectly, but I could understand the purpose of the lecture. Every book I bought in the Saint Mary's bookstore I may have opened three or four times at home—either because I was not motivated or because I never really spent time in my apartment. The social aspect of school was fine; I was meeting lots of people. As soon as I approached someone, he or she would talk my ear off. It was hard to listen sometimes, but I tried.

Even though classes were becoming easier, my abilities were not going toward tests and essays. All I could think about were the light, the blank page, and the sense of an instant eternity.

During many of my classes, I would doze off, reaching into my vision, trying to make out the message: Write a book about Oak Island. Coming back to what was real, I noticed some of my classmates turn their heads again, trying not to be recognized. People knew me, but I didn't know them. The only way to relax now was to go to Jesse's in the evening.

One more class, more eyes staring, more revelations.

I took the bus home and ate my supper, some rubber stuff in the microwave. Jesse's apartment in Clayton Park was about a twenty minute bus ride from my place. I entered the apartment, and I knew from the smell in the air that Mary Jane had arrived. The apartment had a huge, white living room with a skylight, two bedrooms, a huge closet, and a quaint, little kitchen. This was my first university career: Go to school, go home, go to Jesse's, see Mary Jane.

Jesse lived with his sister, Rebecca, and Brad Fisher, Kirk's younger brother. Brad was shy but if you asked him to do something he would. He was a Fisher. We sat; I smoked. Mary Jane was there. Everyone was happy.

"I love this shit," Brad said.

"What is love to you guys?" I said.

Everyone was quiet, nobody knew what to say, not even Rebecca, who looked at me rubbing her nose.

"Boys, you may not know love when you got it, but you definitely know when you don't have it."

"Words to live by," Rebecca said, walking into the kitchen.

All I was thinking about was a woman, but right then I had Mary Jane. I smoked the stars higher, the clouds all around me, these clouds I thought were now mine. My eyes were like the two of diamonds. Mary Jane smelled so good. The next morning, I went back to school, the library, to piece together parts of history that were not totally lost but had been forgotten. There was a book I was drawn to, attracted to, something I needed to read. The book was called *Atlantis.* I borrowed the book and started to read it, sitting by a tree in the middle of the quad.

The more days went by, the fewer people said hello, which made me more comfortable. It was like I had a new home, a place that accepted with paper, now with people, Saint Mary's University.

I was going broke because I was spending too much time with Mary Jane and cigarettes. I needed money. I went to see Jesse and asked for help.

28. TREES

Bacon, eggs, toast. The smell of breakfast is a call few can miss, especially before work. I could smell the meal but I didn't really want to get up. I knew what was in store.

"C'mon, Pelley, no time to be lazy," Jesse said; he probably already had his work clothes on.

I sat up and scratched my eyes. I couldn't see the Edisons' basement because it was black; there were no windows or openings to the outside, just stairs leading to the door. I felt around to get my clothes and headed upstairs. It was a home-style breakfast; usually whenever guests, company, or friends were in the house, the best meal of all followed. Although eating was good, there was no time to waste when it came to the family business, selling Christmas trees. This year, since I, like Jesse, was a student with no money, Abe hired me for the job.

I jumped in the back of the old pickup truck, and we left Middlewood. Buck was with me. We took an old junction off Highway 103.It was chilly for a late fall day, the wind biting my face, the cold crushing my fingers even though I wore gloves and proper clothing for the season. Buck looked ready for this, like he loved running around the Christmas tree lot more than a golden milk bone; the chill did not bother him, his tongue was flapping with the wind.

We turned off the road, onto a self-made drag. Getting stuck wouldn't have been a surprise. The more bumps in the road, the closer we got to the lot. It looked as though there were a thousand Christmas trees as far as the eye roamed. It smelled like the kind of Christmas that would wake children up at five o' clock in the morning. We finally reached the camp where Abe wanted to start; certain trees were marked due to their maturity. After I had a smoke and Abe had a cup of tea, we did the same thing we'd done the day before. Abe found a tree and cut it with his handy chainsaw. Jesse and I hauled the tree to the road, sometimes over a credible distance. Later the binding machine would tighten the tree with twine, getting it ready to send to people so they could celebrate the birth of Christ. If Buck could have hauled all the trees by himself, the smart dog would have.

Christmas tree work is the hardest work I have ever done in my life. After a couple of hours hauling trees to the roads, binding, and throwing them onto the truck, the sweat would start leaking through my sweater, so much sweat a glaze started to show on my hat.

After half the day was done, we took out our lunches. Abe drank his tea, Jesse ate a sandwich, I smoked a cigarette.

"How are you doing, Pelley?" Abe said, not knowing if I could keep up with the strenuous work.

"I don't know, but out here, more than anywhere else, I feel close to God."

If you could hear the clouds coming together, forming, you would out here. If you could see and hear every Christmas tree grow, you would out here. If you could hear the animals sleeping for the winter, their hearts beating slowly, you would out here.

Nature had started to dream; one day, it would waken again.

"Well, can't waste time," Abe said.

We went back to work. Sweated, hauled, bound, put trees on the truck. After a long day, it was time to go back to Middlewood. The four of us squeezed into the cab and headed back to the house. I thought the day was over, but we had to unload the trees off of the truck. Still, it didn't take Jesse and me long to take the last tree and lean it by the others. Sore and fatigued, we all had a couple of beers, satisfied with the work that had been done.

We had to head back to university soon, so Abe paid us for our time with the trees. For all that hard work and God's intended creation, nature itself, I made enough money to have a real good time with Mary Jane.

29. CABIN

The three of us—Kirk, Jesse, and I—were overwhelmed in Halifax. Kirk was living with Jesse. Brad had gone off on other endeavors; he was a young man who was looking for a job to satisfy his parents' nagging and his empty pockets. Jesse was looking to do well at school, to see that his lifetime goal to be a teacher became a reality. For me, every step I was taking, whether in school or being alone in that apartment, was toward a place of peace. All of us needed peace, without traffic lights and twenty-four-hour convenience stores.

"What should we do?" Kirk asked.

"Go home," Jesse said. He meant that we should return to a smaller town with the same things I wanted to escape.

"What about the cabin?" I suggested.

I think they knew saying no would be futile.

"We'll have to pick up some things," I said, referring to Mary Jane and some magic mushrooms. I hadn't done any magic since the night I saw the blank page. I never thought that vision would happen again.

"All right, but do you think we will get back there?" Kirk said. Snow had fallen a couple of nights before, although it was a clear and crisp February day.

"The road will be plowed, I just hope the cabin is all right," Jesse said.

With that, we headed to Kingsburg, Rose Bay, away from resumes, books, and the network of civilization. The first time I ever went out to the cabin, there had been four of us. Joshua, myself, Kyle, and Coles. Coles was our leader that day. He had hitchhiked to the cabin before. Oh, and how can I forget Mary Jane. I spent many days of my fourth year of high school with Kyle, going into the woods by Parkview, smoking Mary Jane until she was gone.

Coles was a big man with short blonde hair and the greatest smile in the world. If you were his buddy, you had no worries. If you were his enemy, you'd run.

Once when we were all at the cabin, Coles took us out to the rolling fields near the edge of the cliffs.

"Lay down, boys," Coles said. "If you see a shooting star make a wish." The sky looked like there was salt sprinkled over the dark; there were so many stars you could lie there forever and just be in awe. Then there it was, the shooting star, streaking left across the sky. My wish was simple: nothing more than a kiss. My wish was that I would have a woman someday. We watched the stars, all of them.

After that trip, I told many friends about the cabin, especially Jesse and Kirk. With many trips made to Kingsburg, it became a place of refuge.

We drove from Halifax to Middlewood in decent time. Jesse borrowed his parents' car so we could make the trip. The roads, to our surprise, were not slippery, that is, until we reached the steep, rocky way leading to the cabin. Our prayers kept us going: Please let us make it, please let us make it. We made it, four tires bringing us the hope of serene splendor for one night.

We got the things we needed from the car—sleeping bags, food, playing cards, axes, cigarettes, lighters, magic mushrooms, and Mary Jane—and headed down the path. We knew the woven path, but we had never been out there at this time of year. Everything was white, snow on the balsam fir branches, ice finding its way on to shore, the tide crashing on the cliffs like milk splashing out of a glass, and more ice on the path. We had to take more precautions than ever before. One wrong step, and the cold, raw ocean could claim us. We noticed a tree on the path, hanging on to its survival by its roots. We ducked under and continued to walk; some steps were treacherous.

Our worries about the cabin's condition were soothed when we came upon the old, gray structure. We dropped off our things and went out to the cliffs where I'd made that shooting star wish. The Nova Scotia shoreline kept its beauty and majesty. You cannot take it; just share. We were glad we'd finally made it.

"We need some wood for the fire," Kirk said.

We took out the axes and started cutting some trees. For some reason, maybe because I grew up with an electrical fire place and didn't know the first thing about what kind of wood would burn, I started to hack away on a petrified tree. It was like hitting a baseball bat on a steel pole. I think the boys knew what I was doing, but they continued watching me hack on that petrified tree for the joke, so they could laugh.

"How you doin', Pelley?"

"All right," I said, continuing an act there was no use in starting.

The boys finally had enough wood cut for the night; we went inside to keep warm. With bellies full from macaroni and cheese made on the cast-iron stove and Mary Jane filling the cabin, Kirk decided to make some tea, magic tea. I was all for it. The magic floated to the top; I could see it in the tea.

"Down the hatch, boys," I said as the hot, putrid-tasting tea went down my throat and settled at the top of my stomach. I knew the magic took a while for its spell to start, so I was patient. I had dealt with magic before.

"You guys wanna play whist?" Jesse asked.

"Guaranteed," I agreed.

Three-handed whist has the same principle as the game for four except you play for yourself. Five is a book. Bid over five. Before we started, Mary Jane had to have her part in the game. I smoked. We started playing cards.

The longer the card game went on, the more the magic took over my body. We had moved up to the loft, smoking cigarettes and some more Mary Jane.

"Pelley, your go," Jesse said.

I seemed to be in a photograph; I couldn't think, speak, or move.

"Pelley, go."

I saw the card but couldn't play it. I played a card that made no sense at all.

"Pelley! Are you okay?" asked Jesse.

"Come down to the table. We will help you," Kirk said. Both of them were now very concerned. They helped me down the ladder and I sat at the table, looking out the window, facing into the darkness outside. I saw a shimmer of light glide out of my right eye then curve upward to the right, toward the ceiling, toward the sky.

Instant eternity.

The light.

A blank page.

I regained awareness and I thought revelation, but it left me, like a dream that was real. It was like talking to the Almighty for an eternity that lasted a split second. It was like hugging my own soul or seeing it from an infinite distance away. Time is an invention of man, with an original outline by God. My vision was divine. The experience gave me the same message the first Adam was given. With meaning, deliberation, and reasoning over time, the message was that I had done something very wrong, but I could be forgiven. I just could not eat from the tree of life like the first man had done.

I was not sitting where the vision began but on the other side of the table when I woke up.

"Pelley, Pelley, you all right?" Jesse said.

"Yeah, I thought something, yeah, but I'm cold," I said. I was cold not from the weather but from the inside—again, it was something divine.

Kirk was really startled, and he started to get sick. He ran out of the cabin and went into the woods.

"Pelley, lie down, and I'll give you some sleeping bags," Jesse said. Now he had two people to look after, myself in a misunderstood dazzle and Kirk in a misunderstood emergency.

"I'm cold, yes," I said. I couldn't speak much; I felt something of immense proportion had just happened not only to me but the three of us. I lay down, cold but with my mind clear. Jesse went to check on Kirk. If Jesse had not kept his composure that night, my words would not be written, my friends' words not spoken.

We woke up in the morning and before anything was done I took a pencil and wrote in the wood of the cabin: "THE WORLD HAS CHANGED." I wrote it for no reason. We grabbed our things and left, hearing the crashing of waves, a noise that reminded us of the incident that almost took our lives the previous night. We watched our steps, ducked under the tree, and made sure we got back to Jesse's parents' vehicle, our way to the society we wished we'd never left.

"Boys," Jesse said, "We are never gonna tell anyone about what happened last night. All right?"

Kirk and I agreed. Even though I have written these words, I hope my friends forgive me.

30. COLLAPSE

When I got back to Halifax, everything was different. Classrooms felt larger, my stride longer, the wind sweeter. Even when I got back to my apartment, it felt cleaner, but it wasn't. There were many things on my mind, one more than others: I was searching for the eyes of Madonna. Those eyes would give me comfort, make my mission complete. I went to philosophy class and in front of me, three times a week, was a red-haired girl who loved the color purple. She wore purple clothes, she had purple pens, but I think she didn't want to share her eyes.

Wherever I went, I looked for the eyes. Some were nice but were not those of Madonna. I started to think of the past, the night where time had no meaning. Why did this vision happen to me? I left class and headed for the Tower. I became a little paranoid; people seemed to be looking at me as if they were searching for someone who was familiar only through gossip.

"Hey, Adam."

I turned around and I saw Seth, my former classmate from Parkview, now a Saint Mary's freshman.

"How are you doing?"

"Okay. This weekend was a little weird."

"Why?"

"Well, everyone wasn't themselves. It was just different."

I thought back to Rose Bay, the blank page. I think now that maybe it was not only the three of us who felt that heavenly moment. The whole planet shook, every person captured its holy essence.

"Is everything all right?"

"Yeah, everybody's fine now. Well, gotta go to class," Seth said, heading off in his clumsy walk.

With school finished, I got on the bus to go to my apartment. More eyes were looking at me, but I was looking for the eyes of Madonna. I went to my apartment, ate some cheap microwavable food dish, and headed up to Jesse's.

As I entered the Edison apartment, I again knew that Mary Jane had arrived.

"Hi, Pelley," said Rebecca.

Rebecca's eyes were like a heavenly body within themselves, but she had her ways, was in love with another. Still, I had dreams.

"What's up?"

We sat around, Jesse, Kirk, Rebecca, and I, enjoying old wrestling tapes, particularly Ric Flair. The Four Horsemen put the stamp on what professional wrestling is today, but that's another story. The more the Ric Flair chopped someone's chest, the more I thought about the light at Rose Bay. I smoked more and more, Mary Jane filled my head as she filled the room. I felt like I was turning back into a photo.

"I gotta use the washroom," I said.

I walked down the hall and collapsed. Then, there was nothing. After there is the light, everything, there is the dark, nothing. That's the only way to describe it, the only way to define it: nothing.

"Pelley, you all right?" Jesse asked with urgency.

"I think so. I don't think I can smoke weed anymore."

"It's up to you," Jesse said.

"I agree," Rebecca countered.

I sat there on my ass, hands joined on my knees. I thought it would be the last time I would have smoke Mary Jane. Little did I know that thought would turn my world upside down.

31. BOWLING

I was sitting in my apartment, smoking cigarettes. I was too lazy to open my school books. I was too lazy to do any cleaning. I was watching one of the three channels that actually came in on the small television my grandmother gave me when I heard my buzzer ring. It was Evan.

I quickly picked up things on the floor, tidied the apartment, and made it look like a place with some sort of order, not a waste of lonely peril. I opened the door before he knocked. "What's up buddy," I said as I welcomed him.

"Not much. I can't stay long, but what are you doing tonight?"

"Nothing. You see it."

"Do you want to go bowling?"

"Sure, with whom?"

"Myself, Heather, and Andrea."

"Cool, but do me a favor. Pick something up." Mary Jane was still in my thoughts; I couldn't flee from something that had become part of me.

"All right," Evan said, as he let himself out.

Andrea was a younger girl, with a beauty that made your jaw drop to the floor; an eagle could fly right into it. She had a cute face and a sweet voice. I had met her a few times over at Evan's apartment and had a couple of conversations with her. I cleaned myself, head to toe. I wanted to be fresh yet not overly strong. I prepared the apartment for company.

When the buzzer rang, I was ready. Evan came in with Heather; Andrea was not far behind.

"Well, let's get started," I said,

Mary Jane was in my hands again. I never wanted her to leave. I wrapped her; I smoked. We were having great talk about good times; the girls had their gossip. Then Heather started talking about a homosexual we all knew; then she looked at me, grinning with her chin tilted sideways. I don't know if I turned white as snow, red as a rose, or the color of the aura I had was coming out of me, but Heather's grin turned into a huge insinuating smile. I thought to myself. This girl thinks that I am a homosexual. Do other people think that? Am I gay?

Evan and Andrea's attention turned toward me; they were looking at me differently than they ever had before. I was anxious. I was not attracted to the same sex, but the thought would not leave my mind. She thinks I am gay. Am I gay?

"Let's go bowling," Evan said, who wanted to get out of the situation as quickly as possible.

We got into Evan's car and went to the bowling alley. Not many words were said, but the thought kept echoing in my head: Am I gay? As we entered the alley, people looked as if I was red or white, different from anyone else in the glow in the dark lanes.

Bowling: the pins of perception, the alleys of always, the balls of bewilderment.

The more I thought, the more people would stare. Did they know me? Could they hear my thoughts? Am I gay? All eyes were upon me. I started to get the sensation that it wasn't what I was wearing or how I carried myself, but that people were perceiving the words coming out of my head. The only thing that could take my mind off the paranoia was Andrea. She was beautiful. But the more people looked at me, the more the question skipped through me. Am I gay?

I went to the washroom and ran into an old football teammate from Saint Pat's. I don't think he wanted to be seen with me. We talked for fifteen seconds. I felt like I was in his head. I couldn't bowl. My stride was off with all the commotion of spirit and sense. How could someone read your mind? It felt like everyone in the bowling alley could read mine. Evan bowled the best, Andrea was good. My mind wasn't on bowling; it seemed my mind was on a string with everyone else's. There were words on a string that only I couldn't read.

Am I gay?

We got in the car, and Evan drove me home,

"Is it okay if you drive me home, Ev?" Andrea said. She may have had thoughts of coming to my place afterwards, but if she could read my mind that night, she would have been confused.

I went to bed, wondering if reading thoughts could be reality, wondering what it would have been like if Andrea stayed, wondering why people looked at me when I thought.

I woke up and the question hit me like a heavyweight boxing champ's right hand: Am I gay? I knew I wasn't, but that thought created such a great internal reaction, I believe my mind wanted to know if thought-broadcasting was real. I couldn't stop that question. I got ready and caught the bus for school.

Am I gay?

Everyone wanted to look, to peek at me without me noticing, but I saw them spying. My first class that day was philosophy. I got there a little late, sat down, and started thinking. Am I gay? I saw the spirit of the redhead who liked purple shrink; the teacher struggling to get through her class; the guy sitting next to me jumping up and down a little. I knew it. It was real. People could hear my thoughts.

I left the class. The feeling of people reading your mind is powerful at first, and then it turns into a bushel of thorns. You cannot escape it; it is always there. There was only one answer for me after being so uncomfortable with the new reality, particularly since I was broke. I would have to get through the week and go see my mother in Pleasantville; this trip signified a final pleasant goodbye to Mary Jane.

32. CHAMPIONS

I was home, Pleasantville. My mind was like a drag strip with no finish line. I just wanted to rest, and home was my place for peace. My bedroom was in the basement, so I had to walk upstairs to use the washroom or get food. I was half scared. If I told my mother I believed people could read my mind, she would tell me I was crazy, sick. I also couldn't tell her that I was like this because if she knew anything was wrong with her little boy, it would devastate her. She would take me right to the hospital. The other part that scared me was that I believed I had an extra sense, a new ability. I sat down at the kitchen table. Ray always watched television by the table, but if nothing interested him, he played his one-man card game. Ray was lying down so I knew what I wanted to watch.

The Saint Mary's Huskies Basketball Team was in the semifinals of the national championship tournament, which was held every year at the Metro Centre in Halifax, the capital of Canadian basketball. Today, the championship is held elsewhere in the country. The Huskies knocked off the number two ranked Western Mustangs to make it to the semifinal against the Macmaster Marauders.

Saint Mary's was led by that leader of the pack, the former hungry lion, captain by game and by competition, the best player I have ever seen step foot on the Parkview gym floor, the man who captivated me with his raw talent in high school. Now he had led his team to a stage where they were not supposed to be. A team that was fair during the regular season, they ripped through the Atlantic University playoffs, earning a title and a seventh seed out of eight teams in the tournament. The Huskies were true underdogs.

I turned on the television and promptly a timeout was called. As the Saint Mary's players went to their bench, it seemed like they were talking not about the game but about me. Had they heard that gossip in school? Had I passed one of them in the halls of the university? Why would they talk about me when there was a national championship to be won?

"I'm going downstairs, Mom. Tell me if SMU wins."

Mom told me what I believed would happen: Saint Mary's won, making it to the national championship game. There was no way I was going to miss that game.

"Mom, I'm going back to the city early to watch the game."

"Tomorrow on the bus?"

"Yup."

Many nights previous to this one, noises and voices had started to jump through my head. One in particular was female. I was convinced this voice came from physical means, a beating body. I imagined a woman who was famous, adored, someone to whom I could talk forever because of the way she spoke. Someone I could look at forever because even her frown would be like a smile, would make me smile. Her eyes, her lips, her hair.

"Are you Drew Barrymore?"

"Yes," the voice said.

When I wanted to talk she would disappear from my thoughts, speaking when I felt alone or frightened by the feeling of my new existence. She would come, but not long afterward she would leave. When she was gone, it was not long before she would come again. She would not say much because there was not much to say. I didn't think she had much time for me. Sleep started to become worse, a cracked memory.

I woke up in the morning, and mom had my favorite: cheese omelet. She sensed something was wrong, but she probably thought it was just another phase, especially as I was then in my young college days. I gathered some clothes and got some money from Mom, who was managing my finances, and said good bye to Ray. Mom drove me to the bus in Bridgewater,

"You be good."

"Yes, Mom."

I had been riding the bus since I was six years old, back and forth, on the old highway and Highway 103 to see my dad, who lived in Halifax. When I was younger, living in Stonehurst, I caught the bus in Lunenburg. I would rather have made the straight drive through in a car. But sometimes the scenery of Mahone Bay and Chester reminded me that this was where I was from.

The bus driver let me off near my apartment. I dropped everything and called a cab to take me to the game.

"Where are you going?" the cab driver politely asked.

"Metro Centre. SMU is playing for the national championship"

"Yes I know, I know," the cab driver said, "Who is going to win?"

"Saint Mary's," I responded.

"How do you know?" A baffled look crossed his face.

"I don't," I answered, with the same baffled look.

I paid the cab driver and went to the booth to pay for my ticket. Finally, I had my ticket to the show. The national championship. The Saint Mary's Huskies versus The Alberta Golden Bears.

Champions: the pinnacle of play, the desire of dreams, the conclusion of competition.

As I walked up the stairs to the arena, it was like my heart was on a rubber band, throwing itself out of my shirt than back again, over and over.

"How are you?" Alice asked, coming up the stairs behind me. She was a girl I knew from Bridgewater, stunning and vibrant.

"Fine, yourself?"

"You sure everything is okay?"

"I think so."

She patted me on the back and walked off, as I made it up more stairs and entered the playing arena. The orange seats in the Halifax Metro Centre had turned into a circle of life, unbroken and together to cheer for their hometown Huskies. I made my way to my seat, section thirty-six, halfway up, the nosebleed section. As I walked up the upper bowl, I heard a familiar voice,

"Pelley," said Michael, my former Irish teammate.

"Hey, what's up?" I acknowledged him.

"It's going to be a good game."

"Yup."

"Think SMU is gonna win?"

"I don't know."

I continued to my seat and relaxed. I grasped the notion that since I was all the way up there, not many people could hear my thoughts; only the few that were sitting around me near the top of section thirty-six. I was glad my seat was up there. My paranoia lifted from my shoulders a little. As the two teams warmed up, the way they usually did before any game, the music, the sound, beat like a heart that was settling down my own. I was now ready for the national championship.

For a game that was made up of runs, this game was back and forth, basket for basket. Alberta got to its biggest lead of seven points, but with will and approximately nine thousand people behind them, Saint Mary's made their way back. The teams' sneakers on the hard-wood court sounded like hungry rats in distress. All they wanted was the score, the hoop was their dish, the court was their table, the ball was their bite, all culminating in that competitive grace, the way the points made music in the net. With the SMU players trading baskets and depending on tough defense to keep them into the game, they came back and took a small lead. At the end of the first half, the Canadian final was tied 36–36.

This national championship would be determined in twenty minutes.

The energy in the Metro Centre was incredible; spectators were excited about anything the Saint Mary's Huskies did. With every rebound by a SMU forward, the crowd went crazy. With every basket scored by a SMU center, the crowd went crazy. With every three-point shot made by a SMU guard, the crowd went crazy. Everything the captain did—hustle, steal, rebound, score—the crowd went crazy. But when the Golden Bears scored, the Metro Centre went silent, except for the University of Alberta's few supporters. The game seemed to turn into an irregular heartbeat.

A Golden Bear brought the ball up the floor; the former Lion, now Husky captain was guarding him. Steal the ball, I thought to the captain. He went to steal the ball; it went off the Alberta guard's leg and went out of bounds. I thought that nine thousand people could hear my thoughts. The game went back and forth; nobody could go on a run. Alberta tied the game, 61–61, with a little over thirty seconds left.

The ball was in the hands of the captain. With no time left, he missed a leaning jumper, sending the 1999 national championship into overtime. I could see the Saint Mary's coach talking to his team. Maybe he was talking to them about the 1979 (the year I was born) championship at SMU, when he was a student: the hard work, the sacrifice with sweat, and how they could accomplish this feat like he did. Or perhaps he told them to forget about that win altogether, that this was their time, their time to win the banner.

Overtime wasn't any different than regulation, with the teams trading baskets for the first four minutes. But with a little luck, some cool but nervous foul shooting at the end and doing things right when it counted, the Saint Mary's Huskies were named national champions. A miracle in my mind, a miracle for whoever loves the game.

SMU students filled the court, jumping up and down in jubilation. I sat with a smile on my face, taking everything in.

"Need a ride home?" Michael asked.

"No, I'm okay," I said.

The Husky captain received the trophy and held it up toward me, as if I'd helped them on their road to victory. What did I do? My mind was going faster than the up-tempo game I'd just watched. I had done nothing. Through heart, hustle and help from the people of Halifax, the Huskies proved by hard work alone they were the best and earned it.

I got a cab back to the apartment. I was tired so I turned on the television before going to bed. Mike Bullard was on the tube, Canada's version of David Letterman. I thought to myself, How powerful could this ESP be?

"Hello, can you feel that wind, can you hear me?" Mike Bullard said.

An idea ran through my mind that everyone from Halifax to Toronto could hear my thoughts; later, I'd come to believe that everyone could hear them through the television as well.

33. TELEVISION

I was sitting in my apartment. I was beyond paranoid. I had no security of self. The race in my head had now turned into a small conflict; my hope was that all the struggles would end. The physical struggle to leave my apartment without distraction. The mental struggle to make things right in my mind again. The spiritual struggle, the search for what is and what will always be. I wanted all the struggles to turn into silent sentiment; the only thing now that could change all things were the eyes, the eyes of Madonna.

I had to go to school; it was what I was in the city to do. I would always just catch the seventeen bus to Saint Mary's by Bayers Road Shopping Centre, or miss it by mere seconds. Once I got on the bus, it seemed that I was inside of everyone, floating into their senses, diving into their minds. In turn, the thoughts of those people somehow were attaching themselves to me.

Attending school became harder and harder. The string of words became a chain, a link so heavy that understanding reality started to become more difficult than understanding lessons in a classroom. My reality was so difficult that everyone would look and not speak, glance and then shy away. My only relief was the search, searching for the eyes of Madonna.

I went to my philosophy class and I couldn't pay attention. I could listen only to the fight in my mind. A, E, I, O. The more the teacher spoke, the more the students reacted to my thoughts. If I thought something crude and careless, they would shift and slump in their seats. If I thought something positive, they would straighten up, wanting more. The start of war, a glimpse of divided essence.

It was becoming too much. There were people staring at me in the cafeteria, laughing and snickering in the hallways. I was paranoia to the people. Where were those eyes?

I went to the smoking room in the student union building and lit a cigarette while taking out a book. I smoked, wandering off from my words, thinking about what I could do to break free from my fright, students invading my mind.

Basketball.

Epiphany in a lonesome soul is earth trembling.

I packed up my smokes, put my book in my bag and got on the bus, waiting for tomorrow so I could go to the Tower, the SMU athletic facility, to play the sport I loved. I was alone, by choice. Or perhaps the choices I had made in life had left me to waste away in my apartment. Either way, I was alone. I called Jesse to see what he was doing. He told me to come to his place; Kirk had joined him.

The boys were relaxed, ready for an evening of company and cards. Jesse was in control of the television remote when he came upon a basketball game, the Phoenix Suns versus the Minnesota Timberwolves. As Jesse put the remote down, the whole game we were watching halted, stopped. It was a team or official timeout, or an extraordinary happening for those at the basketball environment, a gigantic twenty-thousand seat structure, for us a twenty-four-inch screen. The players for both teams were pointing up to the ceiling of the building, the heavens, as if they heard a voice coming from above. The more I thought, the more the players on the court reacted. The game became disorganized, like my mind had been all day. I felt Jesse and Kirk were experiencing the same thing I was, finding it hard to believe what was going on but having to because it was happening right in front of them. All of it. They couldn't look away from the TV; for a second, my thoughts were still. It was like we were there; the game was in the apartment. Reality had another new meaning.

"You guys wanna play some cards?" I said.

"Yup," both of them agreed.

We started playing whist, and Charles Barkley started to get mad, like I was the son of God playing a sinner's game. I thought to him that we were not playing for money, just a friendly game. Charles settled down.

With the television being able to hear my thoughts now, the conflict in my head became more intense. The people on the television didn't understand. Kevin Garnett was really mad at me. We continued to play whist. Kirk always won at the three-handed game. I thanked the boys and went home. None of us had much to say; it was hard for me to use words to describe what had happened.

New experiences brought a new fear that everyone was digging inside of me, stripping me of my confidence. Every thought was public, from the need to take a pee to a crush on a girl on a bus to thinking bad things about a teacher when I got something wrong in class. EVERYTHING. There were no secrets, no self esteem, no self-respect. It felt like the world was on my back. I wanted to cry but couldn't; people's faces suggested they wouldn't cry for me but only generate more gossip about the dissension within me. There was more to me than this, but it seemed to me people didn't care. I couldn't go to class as much as I should have. I'd watch TV, and the shows were built around me, with the actors calling me devil or angel. I knew I wasn't either one. I was the brunt of every late-night joke. I couldn't even watch the great one (Wayne Gretzky) retire like I wanted to because of my mental mess. Television used to be relaxing; now it was torment.

Maybe it was Mary Jane I missed; maybe if I had her, everything would turn back to normal. Or maybe it was Mary Jane herself that had caused the chaos inside of me. All that mattered now was the eyes of Madonna. I didn't get to play basketball. The conflict in my mind was now an all-out war that went through me, penetrated me; it was never ceasing. I had started to change in many ways that were hard to comprehend. I wondered whether other things in my world were going to change too.

34. COLUMBINE

It was my last class, not that the school year was officially over, but I was like a shining affliction for everyone to see, the focus of every classroom. It was too hard; I couldn't sit through class. The words in my head were becoming missiles, my ideas were bottled-up bombs, silent explosions of darkness. This war was becoming too much for me; I couldn't even walk on the sidewalk. My apartment was a trench where I could hide from my enemy. My enemy was myself.

Ever since I had my overcoming blissful experience, I would say this phrase to my friends, even though I didn't understand it: "Everything is nothing, nothing is everything."

The war continued. I walked into the gas station by my apartment to get some soda and pick up the newspaper. The soda was the same, Pepsi, but the paper was shocking. HIGH SCHOOL SHOOTING IN COLUMBINE, COLORADO. As I looked at the front page, I thought to myself maybe I could change this. Time is an invention of man, with an original outline by God.

I looked at the gas attendant and thought to him that perhaps I could do something about this tragedy. It seemed like he agreed, nodding yes back to me. Walking feverishly back to my apartment, I laid out my plan. I would watch a show that had been taped before the Columbine High School shooting. The actors, directors, and producers would hear my warning and, hopefully, go to the proper officials and stop the people that created the horrific point in time. I waited until about mid evening and turned my television to a show called, *Ally McBeal*.

I thought everything to them: what had happened, who the suspects were. I read straight from the newspaper about the events that had destroyed so many lives. I couldn't tell from the show if the actors were receiving my message or not. All I could think was how tremendous it would be to save those lives, to bring families back together, to make a community strong and alive again once more.

The war continued. I placed the newspaper on the floor in front of me; if my part was done, when I woke up the headlines on the front page would have changed. As I anxiously tried to go to sleep, I heard a voice with a high tone, mystical and angelic,

"You're breaking the system."

I didn't want to break anything; I wanted to help. It was the most soulful voice I have ever heard. I will never forget it. I smoked a cigarette and closed my eyes, hoping that what I thought was right would be confirmed in ink in the morning. When I woke up, I looked at the paper: same headline, no change, nothing. I didn't know if I should keep trying to save the students of Columbine or whether that would break some sort of system that had to stay intact.

God bless all the people who were affected and who still grieve in Columbine, Colorado.

The war continued. Everything is nothing, nothing is everything. I only went back to school to do my exams. I sat in my apartment smoking cigarettes. The road I was on now would only take me home.

35. FIRST DOCTOR

I was out of the city and home in Pleasantville for what I thought would be the summer. I couldn't recognize the outside world, only the inside, the war. Sleep brought peace with dreams of childhood exploration and moments of overcoming all. But when I woke up, the war began.

"Adam, get up. We're going uptown to look for a job," Mom yelled, trying to plug some initiative in me. "Get in the shower."

I climbed the stairs; Mom had everything ready for me in the bathroom. I locked the door, took off my clothes, and stared into the mirror. Who was I now? Not the child who needed only a basketball to get by. Not the man who could bring a smile or a blush to anyone suffering through an unreasonable day. Who was I?

I was the silent war, but only I saw the siege overcoming my being. A war of tormented thoughts that was waged only inside of me. Did I choose the war? Yet this war had become me.

For a long time, I stared into the mirror, naked.

"Adam, are you okay?" Mom said.

"What?"

"You've been in the bathroom for forty-five minutes. Have you even been in the shower yet?"

Everything was inside; it was affecting my actions. It was time to come clean with my mother. I couldn't clean myself. I finally got washed, put on some fresh clothing, and went to the kitchen to see my mom.

"There is something wrong with you," she said, before I could speak.

"Mom, I think people can hear my thoughts."

"What are you talking about?"

"Mom, everybody can hear my thoughts."

"That's foolish Adam. Nobody can hear your thoughts."

"I know they can."

"All right, we're going to the hospital."

Mom got on the phone and contacted the psychiatric facility in Bridgewater. She scheduled an appointment as soon as possible. She even called my dad to make sure he would make it to the meeting.

We went to the hospital. It was a hot, cloudless day as if the only ones who should have been at the meeting with me and the doctor were nature and God. At the cafeteria, Mom and I waited for Dad, who was coming from Halifax to support his son. When Mom noticed Dad, I could hear her teeth grinding, as he smiled from brow to brow. My dad noticed me, saw me looking beyond what was in front of me, into the emptiness that was left inside of me because of the war. He'd always seen me happy, joyful. He was worried. His smile disappeared.

"Hello, Mindy."

"Hello, Jack."

This was the first they'd talked to each other face to face in years.

"I have to use the washroom," Mom said. She didn't want to be around Dad; maybe old memories took away what could blossom tomorrow.

"Do you want to sit outside and wait? It's a nice day," Dad said.

"All right," I said.

We went outside and sat at a picnic table. The hospital overlooked the town of Bridgewater, but at the beginning of the conversation we looked at each other. "What's wrong, Adam?" Dad said, looking concerned. He thought his little boy was invincible.

"Dad, I think people can hear my thoughts, right through the television. I don't think it, I know it." Dad looked at me, confused. His open mouth and large eyes confirmed he could not believe the words that came out of his boy.

"Adam, if you can do that, you could probably do anything, like Jesus," he said. "See the church bell across the river. If you're Jesus, you could ring that bell."

Over the past couple of weeks, with the broadcasting of thoughts, between people and through televisions, sometimes I'd thought I could be a higher power. That there was evidence that God did exist. I'd always believed, but after my illuminating experience and my new ability, I thought I could be a part of it too. Maybe I was the Second Coming, the answer to the question of all questions, the truth. Adam being the first, who would be the last? I tried to ring that bell with my mind. But there was no sound, just the heat of the day.

Mom came out and said it was time to go into the outpatient psychiatric department. I went in by myself and sat down. I can't remember if Mom and Dad waited together or if Dad went to visit my grandmother who lived in Bridgewater.

I sat by a man who was under pressure, unstable. He kept talking about being so high at one point, then all of the sudden being so low. He was shaking a little. It seemed like he had a war of his own.

"Adam Pelley."

A nurse called me in to see a doctor. He was a man of African descent, but I cannot remember his name. He was small and balding.

"Hello, Adam"

"Hello, Doctor."

"Okay, tell me what's going on."

"Well sir, I believe people can hear my thoughts through the television."

"Okay, when did this start?"

"A couple of months ago."

"So they are able to read your mind and know what you are thinking."

"Yes."

"How can they do this?"

"They just do, maybe they're supposed to?"

" Okay. What about drugs? Have you done any recently?"

"I used to smoke a lot of marijuana and had some experiences with magic mushrooms."

"How long did you do the mushrooms?"

"A couple of months ago."

"Okay, let's get back to your thoughts. Why are people supposed to hear your thoughts through the television?"

"Because I saw the light, the blank page."

"What is this light you talk about?" The doctor shifted in his seat.

"Love. It's like the birds, when they fly in a flock, they turn in the air in sync because they love to fly; it's their purpose. It's like the fish, when they swim in schools and turn in sync because they love to swim; it's their purpose. It's what they think, the good thought. Love."

The doctor started to loosen the knot on his tie a bit, searching for his next question.

"Have you heard voices or noises that other people can't hear?"

"Yes."

"Are they inside or outside of your head?"

"Inside."

"All right," he paused for a minute, leaning forward.

"I think you may have had a little bit of an overdose of drugs. In a couple of weeks everything will be back to normal. Is that okay, Adam?"

"Can you hear my thoughts?" I asked him, trying to get someone to tell me my truth.

"No, Adam. No one can read your mind."

I felt disappointed, shattered. I thought a man of such education would tell me what I was experiencing was real. He prescribed some sample drugs of risperidone, one and a half milligrams at night.

If my dad had gone anywhere, he was back, and my parents went in to talk to the doctor. When I was leaving, the nurses were all saying one word to each other, hope. My parents finally agreed, face to face, for the first time in a long time. I would go to stay with Dad, so if anything got worse, I could go to the city psychiatric ward, the Abbie Lane facility. What I didn't know is that I was about to confront an entity and a deal that I would never forget.

36. THE NIGHT

The night took everything: the children playing, birds singing and the soberness of the sun. With no clouds on the evening, the sky wide with stars and galaxies yet to be named, there was one thing the night could not take: the heavens. Well, maybe two things; this night may have taken something from me.

We ordered a pizza and brought it back to the Twin Peaks apartment building on Herring Cove Road. The building did not resemble what the name Twin Peaks seemed to offer. My father was having a hard time, financially, but having me soothed his situation, even though I was getting sick, a war behind my eyes.

My dad's apartment was small, a one-bedroom with a small kitchen. He had Internet service, which was new to him. There was a dog chained outside to a doghouse in the neighbor's backyard. It seemed they didn't feed him regularly; he had a ten-foot world.

What really intrigued me was the television because I was part of it. Oprah wore white because she thought I was some sort of savior; the local news guys reacted to my thoughts with sarcasm because they thought I had grown into something evil. Even the pro-wrestlers (the WWE) based their whole show on what I thought. It was a battle between dark and light.

My mind was firing so fast in my head, it was hard to do anything except just sit there and take in the television while the television took in me. There was a lot of sickness in the beginning, sickness that I didn't understand.

I went to bed. Dad gave me his bed and slept on the couch in the living room. I lay there, listening to the voices in my head, Drew Barrymore in particular, but there were so many voices it was starting to scare me. On the cusp of confusion, I had to speak.

"You guys must be the devil because you always show up in the night."

I felt something come out of me, out of the top of my head, and spread throughout the room.

"Adam."

"Are you the devil?"

"Yes."

I sat up on the bed, looking, but he wasn't there. I will never forget that voice, hollow and hard, rumbling from the pit of the abyss. I looked out the window and saw the dog barking, his chain rattling from post that inhibited him from the world.

"Why are you here?"

"You."

"What did I do?"

"You sold your soul!"

Adam, you've committed a terrible sin., You cannot eat from the tree of life, and you will be forgiven.

I could remember being alone in my apartment while I was going to school at Saint Mary's. Pigeons were purring like pussycats on my window. The new thought broadcasts were making me challenge myself, repress my mind. I thought it over and over again: no repression, no repression. Suddenly the war produced a nuclear bomb in my conscience, the devil's words remembered, my lonely moment reminisced. Immediately a flashback to a childhood blunder, a mistake that I should have buried in my being forever.

I could remember when I was ten years old, lying in my granddad's brass bed, so tranquil on Rob's Cove in Stonehurst. Everything was still, serene. There was nothing except for sleep. I was alone. Then I said it without any real thought, pondering, or questioning. I said it. I sold it. I asked to be the most popular person in the world. Nothing happened. I just lay there, alone. Then I thought about what I did and about my belief in Christ and myself.

"I take it back, I take it back. I can do it by myself." I could fulfill my own dreams of being recognized in the world

Nothing happened. It was too late. I had sold it.

"No, no, I didn't sell my soul. I give my soul to God, I give my soul to God," I said. I was scared of the voice that only I could hear, and not through my ears but under my skin, in my bones. Satan would spit into a peddle; an old, small, iron cowboy style of bucket whenever he was mad or flustered, whenever he was angry with me. An awkward feeling of energy would start at the top of my head and then work its way down my whole body to my feet, which I thought was a good thing.

"I feel God protecting me," I said.

Satan spit into the peddle. I now know that the feeling of a good god is the opposite of what came over me that night.

"You are Satan," the voice said.

"How can I be Satan when you are Satan. You are a liar; you're the real Satan."

Satan spit into the peddle.

"I'm not Satan, I'm not Jesus, I'm King of the World," I said.

Satan spit into the peddle.

Our arguing continued all night, becoming more and more intense—me catching him in his lies, him spitting into the peddle. The dog was barking, trying to escape from his chain. I could hear people screaming because they'd be thrown into a bottomless blaze by this devil. He was not taking me. With all of this happening, I wondered if any more powers, God-like powers, would come to me.

I went to the kitchen and poured a small glass of orange juice to see if I could turn it into wine. Satan was still in the bedroom. I thought and thought; I turned my finger in the liquid in the glass, making it swirl. There was no wine. I went to the bathroom and started to fill the tub, thinking I might be able to walk on water,

"Adam, you okay?" Dad said in a half-awake state.

"Fine," I said, not wanting him to know about my ordeal.

When the tub was half full, I tried to walk on the water. My toes felt the same as I tested the water. I put my whole foot in the tub. I could not walk on water. I went back into the bedroom. The devil was still there and would not leave. That night, hell also had its limitations. The dog continued barking. Satan would say stupid things; maybe he was trying to make me say stupid answers. Whenever I caught him in a lie, he would spit, over and over, all night.

"I'm not Satan; I'm not Jesus, king of the world."

Satan spit in the peddle.

Why me, why did I have this experience—talking to Satan, voices in my head I couldn't control. I was about to break down in tears. The sun was coming up; the heated feeling went through my body, from head to toe, once more.

Satan spit in the peddle.

"Later, Adam. Ha, ha, ha!"

"He thought I was Drew Barrymore!" said a woman's voice, the one I had been talking to for months in my head. It sounded like they'd all hopped into a fifty-seven Chevrolet convertible with the top down and driven off, squealing wheels on a pavement I could not see. Likewise, the devil I could not see was gone. I wanted to cry and maybe give up on the war, but then I saw the dog outside of the window, chained to that house. That was all he knew. My life was better than that. I could take my chain with me.

I heard my dad turn on the early morning talk show, *Breakfast Television*. I could hear the show through the walls of the apartment. I thought to the people on the show that I'd talked to the devil last night,

"Did he spit into the peddle?" an older host, Scott Boyd, said.

Yes, I thought back.

"He's demonic."

I couldn't understand what was going on. Did I actually talk to that snake in the beginning of the Bible or the devil that met Jesus in the wilderness?

"I'll be back Adam," Dad said, and he went out for the morning papers and coffee. I went to the living room and started channel surfing. I stopped at a show called *100 Huntley Street*. The man on there was positive: "I tell you, you're Jesus, the pope will tell you you're Jesus." I changed the channel. I was not good enough to be Jesus.

I turned back to *Breakfast Television*, and all the hosts looked at me like I was the devil himself, but I knew I wasn't that bad. I watched television all morning. The longer the morning went on, the more I thought I was king. Dad came home, and I started jumping up and down, delirious,

"Dad, I'm king of the world!"

"I know," he said. Maybe he was in my reality, or maybe I was his whole world. Either way, I was king. He sat down and did some work on the computer as I watched television. The more I watched, the more people concluded I was evil, demonic.

"Do you wanna go for a drive?" Dad asked.

"Sure."

We got into Dad's old crimson-red Reliant K car and headed down toward Herring Cove. I liked driving with my father. When I was very young, he sat me on his lap and told me to take the wheel. I drove for about five seconds before we almost went into a ditch.

Dad stopped at the look off and shut down the car. There weren't many people around.

"Adam, go sit on those rocks down there."

I got out, climbed my way down to the shore and found a nice boulder to sit on. I felt that something was supposed to come to me, maybe a realization that there were no demons on this shore, maybe only God could reach me here. With the drum of the sea, the salt in my nose, and the boulder I sat on, I did not feel awake, I felt alive. I thought I was king, over the ocean, over the sky, over the world.

I climbed my way back up to the car.

"Let's go home, Dad."

When we entered the apartment, I turned on the television. Shaquille O'Neal called me demonic. I changed the channel. Oprah Winfrey was wearing black.

37. ADMITTANCE

For a couple of days, I couldn't sleep. The demonic laughs, like a thousand voices enjoying an ironic comedy, would awake me after two minutes of shut eye, laughing and laughing, as I clutched the Holy Bible to my body. The drugs the doctor in Bridgewater gave me did nothing. My mental war was manifesting into a spiritual one, although not in a physical way.

My Uncle Richard—a true believer in a supreme good architect of the universe, a loving and forgiving God, a worshiper of Jesus Christ—came over to talk to me. He'd heard about my problems from my dad, that people reading or hearing my thoughts. He wanted me to know that everything would be good because God is good and always conquering evil. I believed everything he said. I know that good is supreme; it's just that evil follows behind. With time, the ghosts in my head would turn any man into a wasteland. My mind was already becoming a wasteland. I needed help, and I think my family started to realize it.

"Dad, I think I should go see somebody,"

"Are you okay?" Dad asked, already knowing he was going to ask me to go to the hospital.

"I don't know about tomorrow."

We picked up some things and headed down to the Queen Elizabeth II Hospital Emergency. First, we went to triage to see the extent of the emergency.

"What's your name?" said a lady behind a glass window.

"Adam Jack Pelley."

"Do you have your health card?"

I pulled out my health card; my old identification from when I was sixteen was with it. I noticed the aging around and underneath my eyes and realized even more what my three-year relationship with Mary Jane had done to me. I was a wounded casualty of an inner war looking for help and aid at a hospital.

"How can we help you, Adam?" said an athletic-looking man, dressed for his job in the emergency room.

"I think people can hear my thoughts through the television."

"Do you have the feeling you would harm anyone or yourself."

"The thought of hurting myself has crossed my mind lately."

When you think people listen to your every word that is supposed to be your own, the thought of everything being over may be the only conclusion. But the only answer is to believe in providence, to believe the only answer is to continue living.

"Okay, I'm going to get you in to see the on-site psychiatric nurse tonight. Wait down at emergency B with your father." He turned to my dad. "Can you escort him down there?"

"No problem," Dad said.

It seemed like other people had been waiting for a long time, but they took me right away and sent me for help as soon as possible. Dad and I sat in the emergency room, reading newspapers and magazines. It was hard to get through the paragraphs with the wars, the struggles, the conflicts, the fights of all eternity raging in my head. I needed help, professional help, someone who knew how to bring peace to mental illness. People waiting in the room looked at me like my peers did in school, but then they went back to their reading. Their gazes were more acute, as if something had to be done or they might start to begin a war of their own to ensure something was done about mine.

Dad and I went into a small room furnished with one chair and an uncomfortable two-seat couch. White walls surrounded us. We waited for a while. It was getting late so Dad started to fall asleep. I was jittery; the battle raged. Finally, someone entered the room.

"Hello, Adam. I'm Jennifer, the on-call psychiatric nurse."

Dad jolted awake. I wanted to know what was happening in my body.

"What can I help you with?"

"People are hearing my thoughts, right through the television."

"How do you know this?"

"When I think certain thoughts, people react to them; they move when I think something negative to them. There is a war in my mind, I can't stop it."

"What are these negative thoughts."

"I would rather not share them right now."

The doctor wanted to know as much as possible, but I think she wanted me to be comfortable, so she didn't push the issue.

"Have you ever used any street drugs?" the doctor continued.

"Yes."

"Can I ask what kind of drugs?"

"Marijuana, magic mushrooms, some LSD a while back."

"Okay, Adam, do you hear voices?"

"Yes."

"Are they inside or outside of your head?"

"Inside."

"What do they sound like?"

"Some sound like normal voices, some sound like demons laughing."

"Do these demons say anything to you?"

"No, he drove off."

The nurse looked at me as if she knew who "he" was.

"Do you feel like you are going to harm yourself or others?"

"Maybe myself, but I wish no harm upon any living being."

"Okay, I'll be right back," Jennifer said.

Dad looked at me in disbelief. Demons? "You will be all right, my son," he said, always looking for the positive. The positive in this case was that I was breathing. Jennifer walked back into the room,

"Adam we are going to admit you to the psychiatric ward here tonight. We feel you need help in getting control in your developing illness. Is that all right with you guys?"

I had to say yes; my bones were getting sick from the laughs. With hope and help, the demons would hide forever.

"Sounds all right to me," Dad said.

"Let's do it," I said

Before Jennifer left, but after she shook our hands, I had to ask her, "Jennifer, can you hear what I am thinking?"

"Sorry, Adam, but no."

An orderly came and put me in a wheelchair.

"I'll call you in the morning," Dad said.

"Can you call Mom?" I asked.

"Sure,"

The orderly pushed me over to the Abbie J. Lane building. Abbie Lane: the bandage to brain, the stitch for sick, the help to heal. I got up there, and it was late, so they sent me right to bed, giving me sleep medication because the demons would not let me rest. I got into my bed, and it felt like it was swaying, like I was in a hammock.

38. DR. D

"Adam. Adam."

I woke up to see a woman with a bucket of needles in her hand. The white coat she wore made me realize I had nothing to worry about.

"I need to take a sample of your blood. When was your birthday?"

"June 6, 1979," I mumbled, still thinking about the dream I had the night before—Spielberg with dolphins. I didn't know if I wanted to get up or not. I was in a psychiatric hospital; I had never heard anything good about them. Would there be people running around with underwear on their heads? Would someone try to attack me?

I walked out into the hall and realized that this place was usually under control, placid. The walls were painted a very pale pink with blue trim, decorated with pictures of children, making me think of my own younger years when there wasn't an illness. Robbie chasing any car that drove down the sandy road of Stonehurst, running down the hill to greet me when I got home from school.

I couldn't hear the demons anymore; there was only that female voice, the one I thought was Drew Barrymore but was not, sitting in my head, like a lone dandelion in a field, a weed.

"You're Satan, you're gay," she would repeat all the time. I knew I was neither. Sometimes she was joined by other female voices, telling lies to my conscience. The war continued. I walked up to the nurse's station to see if I could get some medication.

"Hello, Adam, I'm Marie. I'll be you're nurse. Here are your medications."

I took the little white pills; they toned down some things but not enough for words to untangle in my head.

"Marie, can you hear my thoughts?"

"Uhhh … no, that's impossible, no one can hear thoughts."

I felt like she was lying to me. Everybody lied, for my own good. If someone did tell me they could hear my thoughts, what would that change? But I had to know if all of this was real. I went down to the smoking room to have a cigarette. This little room shut me off from the universe. When I smoked, I was letting go from all thoughts, a cease-fire to my war.

After I walked out, I looked into the office of the psychiatrist; his name was on the side of the door, David Whynot. I walked back to my room to take a nap; a man was shuffling his feet toward me with his head down.

"Excuse me, can you hear what I'm thinking?"

"No," he said, as he kept shuffling by me.

I went back to my bed, tired due to the sleep medication, tired from just having my eyes open.

"Adam, can you come see the doctor now?" Marie asked, before I could lie down, holding her hands in front of her.

"Sure," I said.

Marie led me into the doctor's office, and there sitting in his chair, with a nice white-collared shirt and black pants, was Dr. David Whynot.

"Hello, I'm Dr. David Whynot, but everyone calls me Dr. D." He put his hand out to shake mine.

"Hello, I am Adam." I shook his hand. His handshake was light but assured. My first impression was that I could trust him.

"So where can we start. How are you feeling today?"

I didn't know what to say; I was frightened because I was in a mental hospital, afraid because I didn't know anyone in the ward, and mad because I thought he knew how I was feeling because he could hear my thoughts.

"Well, I'm in here. I could say better. I could say worse."

"Okay, looking at your admittance report, I see that you believe people can hear your thoughts, that there is some struggle in your mind. How is this done?"

"I think people just have to hear them. I don't know, they just hear them."

"Can people hear your thoughts through the television?"

"Yes."

"Do you have voices inside of your head?"

"Yes."

"Interesting. Does it seem like people talk about you in the street, like they're taking special notice of you?"

"Yes, all the time." I started to feel like he knew me, either by studying me or from a good admission report. Or perhaps he was so great at dealing with the ill that his diagnoses were automatic.

"Is there anybody against you or following you?"

"No."

"Are there ever thoughts in your head that have been put there from the outside, inserted in there?"

"No."

It now felt like that he didn't know me at all, like he was searching for something—not buried treasure but a thorn in the mind. He was just another person who would lie to me.

"Can you tell me about when you first started to think people could hear your thoughts, either face to face or through the television?"

I didn't mention bowling. I thought if I did it would become a main part of what we talked about, and there was no need for that.

"When I saw the light, the blank page."

"And what is this light?"

"God."

"God? Explain."

"Do you have a blank sheet of paper?"

Dr. D went to his desk and grabbed a sheet of blank paper and gave it to me,

"What do you see when you look at this blank page?" I asked.

"Nothing," Dr. D said.

"This is the best way I can describe beyond perfection, God. What if I told you that everything is already there; the pencil is the eraser. Whatever you create, God is already there. God is everywhere. Without the blank page, there would be nothing to create on."

"Interesting," said Dr. D. He leaned forward, clasping his hands, his index fingers on his nose.

"Adam, were you on drugs when you had this vision?"

"Yes, sir."

Dr. D still sat there with his hands together, then leaned back in his chair,

"I think that you have the symptoms of what we would term as schizophrenia," Dr. D. said. "We are going to keep you here, get you on the right medication, and get you on your feet again. Okay? Good."

"Dr. D, can you hear what I am thinking?"

"Adam. It is impossible to hear thoughts. We have to take time and work with your illness." Just what I thought. I got up and shook his hand. I forgot that Marie had been in the office the whole time.

I went back to my bedroom and met my roommate, Rick,

"How are you?" Rick said.

"Fine," I responded. "Can you hear what I'm thinking?"

"No."

I realized that I would be in the hospital for a while.

39. SLEEP

Sleep. All I did was sleep most days, finding peace in dreams rather than reality. At first sleep bothered me, now rest became its own sanctuary. My dreams were different than when I was well; I could control them in some way, seeing or going to places I wanted. This didn't happen often, but it did happen.

I slept because the war was starting to really bother me. Thoughts that I cannot recall polluted my mind to the point that they made me sick. I do not want to show you the way of war.

"Hello, Adam."

A very tall man with glasses, casually dressed, walked into my room,

"My name is Dr. Green. I am a psychiatric intern here. How are you?"

"Okay," I said, waking from a tranquil sleep.

"Do you want to talk about things?"

"Sure."

"What seems to be the problem?"

"I think people can hear my thoughts."

"Huh ... Okay, can you read my mind?"

"No," I said, but that wasn't the problem.

"Then what makes you think people can hear your thoughts."

"I just know."

"Okay, will you be convinced if I think of something, and you can't hear it in my mind, that no one can hear your thoughts?"

"We can try."

He looked at me, his eyes connected to my eyes, like he was trying to project his words,

"Cat," I said.

"No, I was actually thinking house. So you see, no one can hear your thoughts."

Although he made a noble effort, his experiment did nothing for me or my belief in the ability of thought broadcasting. But I thought all the staff wanted good things for me. They knew I was sick, broadcasting or not.

"Thanks, Dr. Green."

"We can talk later."

As soon as he was finished with me, the steel-plated lunch cart made its way down the hall to the dining room: chicken a la king. I noticed that some people ate at a normal pace, but some ate so fast it seemed that they were scared someone would come and take their tray of food. The institution had become part of them. I ate my food at my regular pace.

I went for a cigarette. There were about five of us in the tiny room. "Can any of you guys hear what I am thinking?" I asked everyone. They all looked at me like I needed pills right away, a lot of pills. But they never said anything and kept smoking and puffing.

Only one man, bald and dark skinned, answered me. "What? You think people can hear your head? Do you think you're Jesus or something? Let me see your hands?"

I showed him my hands. On my left hand, there are five lines joining in the center, resembling a star. On my right hand, the lines are not as prominent, but they also join in the center. The man sat back and said nothing; he took another cigarette out of his pack and lit up. He didn't say anything to me while we smoked. I wanted to go back to sleep; my eyes were crying for it. Sleep was a cave where I could pass time until my head was straight.

My father would come in all the time, bringing in pizza and junk food. The one positive thing about the illness is that I had developed a close and stronger relationship with my dad. I called him every night; he would be there if any trouble presented itself. I hope he was not trying to make up for lost time, but now, with Dad and me, time had no limits.

"Adam," Dr. D said.

"Yes."

"Could you come into my office, please."

"Sure." We both sat down and Dr. D wrote something on a piece of paper upon his desk.

"How are you feeling today, Adam? Same as yesterday?"

"Yes, no change."

"What about your thoughts?"

"Same. The war in my head won't stop; it is just constant."

"And through the television?"

"Yes."

"Okay, I don't have much time today, but I wanted to touch base and see if anything had gotten worse. But nothing has changed since you have been admitted."

"Unless you can hear what I'm thinking," I said.

"No one can hear your thoughts, Adam."

I shook Dr. D's hand and started to go to my room. I thought, what if all of this is an illness, that I really was sick? That a deal I made when I was ten made me hallucinate so much that in my mind I was the most popular person in the world. To me, I was. It was my reality, my world, where everyone knew Adam. Sports arenas filled to capacity heard my voice; Hollywood stars knew my every idea; leaders of nations knew my name. Humanity saw my unseen crown. It had to be real; it had to be real. I couldn't accept this was an illness. My reality was just as true as the one everyone else experienced. The world knew me. It had to.

40. TRUTH

I had been hiding something for years, although I think people always knew. It was one thing I had, something I have to this day. It wasn't that I wanted to hide it, but I would get slightly embarrassed about it around my friends. I was going to see the boys today. Joshua, Jesse, Kirk, Smoky, and Evan. The only one who visited me at the hospital was Kirk, who came with his family. I had lived with Fishers one winter when Mom and Ray took the motor home to Florida and another time when Mom and I had some bad times. I didn't know if I could do it, actually say it to someone, this secret I had kept from everyone, the stories I had made up to protect it.

The truth.

When I talked to the boys on the phone, I got the feeling that they didn't want to see me in there. They'd heard the same stories I had about psychiatric wards; they didn't want any crazy people to hurt them in any way. Or maybe they were at the point in their lives where they might think about admitting themselves, and that scared them. I assured them it would be all right, but they still wanted to meet in a place that would be comfortable for all. We decided on the Public Gardens in Halifax. They knew in their hearts I would become healthy once again.

On the day we were to meet, I felt like calling and telling them not to bother coming to the Public Gardens; I wasn't sure I could say what I had to tell them. I went to take a shower, grabbed a towel and a

164

facecloth. As I showered, I wondered how they would react. Would they accept it or laugh? Anyway, I had to tell them. In the same way the water and soap cleaned the dirt from my body, I couldn't hold it in my being much longer. But the only people I could tell were the boys.

The truth.

I lay down in my bed, staring at the ceiling, thinking about telling Dr. D but afraid that it would probably become the focus of our conversation. I thought it may have been the reason I was ill or maybe the reason I was alive.

It was lunchtime: roast-beef sandwiches. As I looked around, it occurred to me that if anybody around here knew my secret, it would spread like pizza dough. Even though we were ill, we were still people. Gossip flooded the halls whenever a new patient was admitted or someone had to be put into the isolation room. If the other patients heard about what I was hiding, it would be the talk of the seventh floor at Abbie Lane for months. Although, since everyone could read my thoughts, maybe they already knew.

I asked for a pass that would allow me to leave Abbie Lane and walked the two minutes to the Public Gardens. The gardens are the heart of Halifax, with flourishing flowers and ponds where hungry birds wait, ready to be fed. It is a tourist treasure. It was as if the sun was sliced open; it seemed to pour out life. The ducks' feathers complemented the bark of the trees, their necks blended with the freshly trimmed grass. I sat under an old tree and waited, taking in the things that were alive, comforted by the fresh grass that was underneath me. With all this abundant new life around—flowers in bloom, creation happening—it was the perfect place to tell the boys what they probably already knew but never made fun of.

The truth

As I sat there, I heard someone come up behind me,

"Pelley ..." Kirk said, knocking my hat off of my head.

The boys were here; the time had come. I started to sweat a little. I wiped my forehead with my arm.

"How's everything goin'?'" asked Jesse.

"Hospital sucks, but I have to be there."

"How long are you going to be in there?" asked Joshua.

"Till they think I'm ready to leave."

The boys didn't say much. It was like they knew I wasn't the old Pelley who would do anything on a dare. I was a man in the middle of a war, somebody who had to get something off his chest.

"Boys, I got something to say," I said. "I gotta come clean with you."

The boys were still, waiting for me to speak.

"Boys, I've never had sex. I'm a virgin."

Adam, you've committed a terrible sin. You cannot eat from the tree of life, and you will be forgiven.

Silence.

The tree of life is the woman's womb, always waiting for the right season, the right time to be harvested, to grow. As the tree matures, it brings life to all it cares for—families, friends, a home—finally, creating life so more life can flourish. Someday I will sit by my tree, but with patience the light will bring me out of the shade.

I think they all knew I was a virgin; they were expecting something more shocking.

"Don't worry about it, Pelley, you will find a woman some day."

"Dude, if I had girlfriend, most of my problems would go away. Or perhaps some problems would start."

After I told the boys, they became more composed, like their old buddy was starting to come back. We walked around the Gardens, taking in the life from the sun, watching families feed the ducks. I had to go back to the hospital; my truth now was that everyone was telling me I was ill, a truth that I couldn't understand.

41. WAR

I slept too much; one nurse started calling me Adam "The Pillow" Pelley. They wanted me to be active. I'd gained about sixty pounds in the six months I had been there, thanks to Dad's pizza treats.

They would wake me up at ten, but I was so sedated with medication, the only thing that would do would make me tired. I would take my pillow and blanket and find an isolated room, curl up in a corner, and sleep some more. Sometimes they would catch me; other times they would let me be. They knew I was having a hard time.

When I wasn't sleeping, I was in the smoke room, the red packaging of du Maurier regular my friend. One time, there were only two of us in there. He stared at me in intense pain, wanting that precious draw off a tailor made cigarette.

"Can you hear what I'm thinking?" I asked him.

"What? No."

I gave him a cigarette.

I was convinced now that every patient that came into the ward had been warned about me, had been told that they could not tell me that I had this ability. The nurses told the cleaners, patients, visitors: "Don't tell him."

I went up to a patient named George, a guy who was my age and skinny; he just didn't seem to belong in a psychiatric institution. I knew him from sitting across the table and eating, chatting in the smoke room, but I'd never asked him the question.

"Hey George, can you hear what I'm thinking?"

George looked at me like he'd just seen a ghost in a car wreck.

"No one can hear your thoughts, that's crazy. Everybody would be pointing at you, talking about you. People would come right up to you and ask if you could read their mind."

Maybe George was right. How could a mind project noise? How could you tell what was inside another man's head? But the idea of broadcasting thoughts was in my nature.

"Wanna go for a smoke?" I asked.

"As long as you stop asking people that question," George said.

I looked at him and laughed. We had some brown-tipped cigarettes. As I sat smoking, Dr. D knocked on the door and gestured to me to come into his office, which was straight across from the smoking room. I wouldn't leave the smoking room unless it was for rest, food, or a book my mother had brought for me. It was called *Mankind* and was by retired professional wrestler Mick Foley. I've loved professional wrestling my whole life but as I have stated before, that is another story. I'd smoke all the time then ask the question to anyone who would be awake and alert, "Can you hear what I'm thinking?'

I walked into Dr. D's office and sat down. He was in his chair, arms across his chest.

"So, Adam, how is everything?"

"No change; the same."

My war had now turned nuclear. I couldn't go near a television or radio. Any type of device with someone on the other end was a pistol of paranoia. All I did was smoke and use the washroom.

"Tell me about your thoughts. What are they like today? Are they different from the last time we talked?"

"Well, the same. When you think people can read your mind, you try to shock them into making them tell you they can with bad thoughts."

"And what are these thoughts."

"I would rather not say. I don't want to scar your soul. These thoughts would not only make you mentally sick but physically sick as well. They are things that strip away life. They give no warmth or comfort. The bad things, the dark side of man; anything that hurts, takes, wants, sucks, never giving to things. Always having for themselves, no thought for others."

"And you think these bad thoughts all the time," Dr. D said, taking a pen from his desk and pressing it to his lips.

"No, Then the good thought will come. Like the meaning of life is to create life, the purpose of life is to grow, every child is a miracle, and we are all in the world so we all are one. The good things, the light of man, anything sharing, caring, providing, helping, loving, do anything you can to produce positive things for people. How all should grow with peace"

With these thoughts, this is the way of war. A war that had changed me into something when I look into the mirror, I may understand some that I see, the space between my teeth when I smile, those full lips waiting for a kiss, but the rest had turned me into something I hate, an illness that has turned my being into a wasteland I can never forget, yet in turn a new man with a Kaleidoscope of eyes and a new realness that I have to learn to love. I was sick, I couldn't see my old self any more, only a mask that I did not recognize.

"And you think like this all the time? Intriguing." Dr. D said.

"These thoughts are like a battle to me, and the broadcast never ends. I think you can even hear my dreams."

"But you know no one can hear your thoughts and that is an illness," Dr. D encouraged, hoping to drive something home.

"What are probably some of the first things broadcasted on radio or television?" I asked.

"You tell me."

"War, since the beginning until now the only one thing that has consistently been broadcasted has been war." There has always been war, from the beginning of time to mythological realm to the conquering of the oceans. Broadcast began with the first newspapers, radio to television and now the internet, through wireless transmissions and satellites and space. War has not only been waged, but the people have known about it."

"And you think this is all true because people can hear your thoughts."

"Maybe I was born into it."

Dr D. sat back. Adam Jack. Adam, the first child of God. Jack, a devil of the sea. Pelley, a disillusioned king with a wasteland of mind, a world within. My name is who I am. Was I chosen for this?

"I think, Adam, that we are going to try some new medication on you. We will slowly take you off the risperidone and put you on olanzapine. Both are anti-psychotics. Very interesting Adam, thank you for your time." Dr. D said, while shaking my hand. He looked at me as if he learned something, tightening his lips and his handshake. He stood up, putting one hand in his pocket.

I walked out of Dr. D's office and straight into the smoking room, and lit a cigarette.

42. EARTH

I was back in again. After being in a closed in environment of pills and sick people, who I started to love because they were in their own reality like I was, they'd let me go live with my dad. But a month later, I came back because I was contemplating harming myself.

They decided to try a new medication: clozapine. I hoped that this one could strangle those voices that I had never seen and turn the nuclear war in my head to something as pleasant as beers with my buddies.

My family was very supportive. My godparents came to see me all the time. My uncle and aunt (not blood relations but children of my godparents) had just had a baby. They would bring her up to the ward, and it would cheer me up. Sometimes, I thought about visiting my godparents, about being a child again, but the war reminded me where I was.

Most of the time, I couldn't go near a television. But there was only one show I watched every Friday night for one hour: Extreme Championship Wrestling. I loved wrestling, particularly Rob Van Dam and Taz. So it was the perfect television show for me to watch. What was hard was realizing what people were telling me: No one could hear my thoughts. No one could hear my thoughts through the television. Nobody—neither the people on the ward nor the wrestlers on the television—talked to me during an ECW broadcast.

Mom and Ray visited as much as they could, but the seventy-five-minute drive was tiresome and expensive for them to do all the time. It was all right. I knew they loved me.

One day, I got a card in the mail from my mother. It was a card that had been specially designed for me. I can't remember what it said on the front, but the small lettering on the back said, "The name Adam is derived from the Hebrew word meaning earth." Epiphany through anything is earth trembling. I didn't know whether to go have a cigarette or to find Dr. D right away.

"Dr. D, Dr. D, I must talk to you," I said.

"Can you wait five minutes?"

"Sure."

I went for a cigarette. My toes were tapping the floor, and my knees were shaking as I sat in the smoke room, a climactic point in time burying into my mind. Just as I was taking my last puff, the doctor summoned me into his office. He did not look happy; he was obviously preoccupied with something disturbing in his work.

"I believe I know my purpose," I said.

From the first time I met Dr. D, I had told him a lot of things—from basketball to drug use. The only things that never came up were the deed and bowling.

"I think I represent the earth."

"Adam, this is a new thing. Can you pass this one off as part of your illness?"

"That's my whole point. I think the whole world is sick."

"Okay, continue."

"We think we are going through evolution as a planet, but we are destroying the same thing that keeps us alive every day. Shouldn't we be doing more about solving global warming and helping people in need? We can talk about the marvelous advances of technology, but there are children in undeveloped countries who are sick because they don't have proper nutrition. When you're sick, don't you try to get better first before you start on new projects? On the other hand, when you look at the earth as a planet, when one side of the earth has the sun shining on it, the other half is dark. I think the earth, the world is schizophrenic itself."

"Can you continue?" asked Dr. D.

"We have light in the dark now, with artificial lights, but we also have dark in the light. People are drinking and doing drugs into the early morning; the atmosphere is filled with industrial smoke. Some cities have so much smog, all of the sun's light can't grace the people on the street. You can't see the stars in the night sky. Evolution is great; like the technology to help sick children, that's light. But people are starving in third-world countries, their needs unmet; that's a huge dark spot on the earth. It has to be fixed so we can truly advance as a species."

"Are you saying there is more dark than light in the world?" Dr. D said, now deeply involved in the conversation.

"No," I said. "I'm saying that we are living in the dark, that we have forgotten about the light, that the world forgot about God."

"But you said you saw the light."

"Maybe I had to be reminded. I think I am saying I forgot about the light too."

Dr. D looked at me, puzzled, yet he had answers. He started smiling, eager for more therapy, as if it were he now in the session.

"So what do we do from here, Adam?"

"Try to find love. I am alone searching, just like the earth." The truth is the earth is a soloist, longing to play for anyone, looking to hold that hand with another. The truth is the earth is alone, everyone looking to the stars for a partner, another planet with intelligent life to call a friend. The truth is the earth is a virgin, longing for a companion, wanting contact with another.

"Adam, you fascinate me, but I think this new medication will work. Give it time and we will see what happens."

"Maybe that's all the earth needs, the right medication. Someone to prescribe it, and everyone to listen."

Dr. D smiled again.

"Thanks, Dr. D.," I said. "Oh, one more thing ... can you hear what I am thinking?"

"Adam, what do you think my answer will be?"

"See ya," I said as I walked out of his office and right into the smoke room, lighting another cigarette.

Two weeks passed and the clozapine started to work. The audible hallucinations went away and the television didn't want to talk much anymore. The hospital released me and put me in a group home. I didn't know how long I would be there or where my spirit would take me.

43. SKI

"Adam, can I tell you something, if you don't mind?" Turner interrupts.

"Sure," Adam says. "You now know about me. I would like to know something about you guys."

Sherri looks repulsed. She just doesn't want to be here. But she wants to support her husband, who was taking in everything Adam said.

"I would like to tell you why we are here, what my dad told me about you."

Adam shifts in his seat, remembering his days of therapy.

It was Christmas, and the Whynots were all at their home in Windsor, Nova Scotia. David took the forty-five-minute commute to work every day while his wife, Debbie, taught classes at an elementary school. Bonnie and Betty, the twins, both went to Dalhousie; one studied history, the other, kinesiology. They got great grades, these were good times; the girls were turning into women. Turner was home from Western University in Ontario, where he was in the first year of his psychiatric degree. He wanted to be like his dad. His dad, his hero. They did everything together. In his younger years, they'd gone to football games at Acadia University and driven into Halifax so Turner could help his dad pick up golf clubs for the spring. But what the family did together and what they enjoyed the most was skiing.

The Martock ski hills were just a few minutes away from the Whynot house. One of Turner's first memories was of his dad trying to teach him on the bunny slopes.

"Everyone gather round the table," David said to his family one day. They were all eager to go to Martock together as a family.

"I am going to ask you guys if you want to do something different this year," David asked.

Everyone looked dumbfounded. Every year, they went skiing nearby.

"How about you guys pack up your things, and we head to Newfoundland and hit the slopes of Marble Mountain."

The girls hugged their father; Debbie covered her face; Turner smiled. They'd always wanted to go to Marble Mountain.

"Well, let's go. I'm ready."

David went upstairs and got his already-packed suitcase. Then he opened the door, and his family saw all their skis on the top of the van, strapped down and secure.

"Go pack. Let's go!"

The drive to North Sydney didn't take long; there, they boarded the ferry to Newfoundland. They took the overnight trip, so they slept most of the way, except for Debbie, who couldn't stand the rough cold Atlantic. David tried to stay up with her, but she told him to sleep, knowing he would have to drive tomorrow.

When they got off the boat, everything was white, from the sky to the pavement. They couldn't see a thing.

"We'll make it," David said, driving slowly, cautious. A two-hour drive turned into a four-hour crawl. Finally, they made it to Hotel Corner Brook; Marble Mountain was just down the road. The scary drive and the bad weather forced the Whynots to wait one more day until they could to do the sport they cherished. The sun spoke to the snow, making their eyes squint and the air soft enough that the hills of Marble Mountain were begging for people to come.

The Whynots paid their skiing fees and went off, for the first time, up the hill. They came down together as one. David looked at Debbie, signaling that this was the time for them to part ways.

"C'mon girls," Debbie said, and the twins went with their mother.

"Turner, let's go," David said, and father and son took the next lift up.

"How's school going?" David asked.

"Excellent, grades are good."

"Do you have a girlfriend yet?"

"Yeah, maybe."

They got off the lift and headed over to the top of the main slope, Country Road, overlooking the Humber River Valley.

"You really want to follow in my footsteps?" David asked his son.

"I want to do it, Dad,"

"There will be a lot of headaches, a lot of them. But seeing people get better is worth all those headaches. Society has placed a stigma on mental illness; people want to lock the sick up and throw away the key. They make jokes and think it could never happen to them. But realize, my son, that most of these people are misunderstood. They actually have a warmth about them. I am glad to say I have the pleasure and the privilege to not only call them my patients, but my friends. There is potential, so much potential in each person that we, as a community, believe are not well. If we could just tap in to this potential, it would make us all better people."

"I think that's why you do it, and maybe that's why I should do it," Turner responded, looking down at his skis.

"But you also must understand," his father continued, "that they are sick, and they have specific needs. Some people have voices in their head that are just as real to them as our conversation right now or the snow under our feet. But, if you really want to be a psychiatrist, you have to do something for me. One of my patients made me realize that everyone experiences his own reality. Some are different than others; most of us have adapted to the same one. All of us want to be in the

same reality, which we should. He will make you believe there is more
to psychiatry than textbooks and medication, but he made me believe
there is something good not only in the mentally ill but inside of me.
His story, his reality is so real to him, it touched me. If you really want
to be a psychiatrist, promise me you will meet this man."

"I'll promise you anything, Dad."

"When we get home, I will give you the address and day when you
can reach him."

"What's his name, Dad?"

"I'll tell you later. Now let's see who can make it down the slope
the fastest."

When they got back to Windsor, David explained to Turner about
Adam. A year later, on a highway that was slick due to overnight
showers, David Whynot died in a car accident on his way to work.
Turner Whynot never forgot about the promise.

Adam looks at Turner. Sherri now is interested because Turner is
speaking about his father. But she hardly pays any attention to Adam,
who scratches his face and clutches his hands in front of him on the
table,

"Your father made me feel once that maybe I did have potential, that
I could do something with my life," Adam says. "And it's nice to see that
your father, my friend, learned something from me. But I am out here
for a reason, and from what I just heard, I believe you are too."

44. TODAY

Happy Friday. I woke up and remember my dream: flying higher and higher then falling, opening my eyes before I hit the ground. I was alone. It was a regular day, due to its schedule, yet somewhat uncertain. Maybe I'd meet some people for the first time and have some good, interesting conversations. I read my morning prayer in the Today booklet, a Christian devotional booklet, then prayed for myself, knees on floor, asking for safety on that day for myself and for those that caused me distress.

I quickly showered, put on some clothes that had been left on the floor from previous wear, and headed out for work, walking up Robie Street to North Street to catch the bus. Robie Street was the site of my home, where I had those fantastic soaring dreams. It's the same street on which my mother gave birth to me, at the Grace Maternity Hospital. My house was green with white trim, like my home in Stonehurst used to be. No hostility, no bitterness, just a go-ahead, an invite to anyone who drops by. Happy Friday.

As I walked to the back of the bus, I saw a woman. Her scent, a fresh shower smell with a hint of peaches, settled my war for a moment, but the spiritual clash of thought continued. Her dress brought curiosity to my mind. Could she be the one for me? I look for Madonna's eyes, but the woman wears fashionable glasses. I would like to talk to her, get to know her, but then I think about my life, my purpose, my promise.

My promise was to wait to wed before I climbed the tree that is the love of a lady, to nest in the heart of a branches sway. Would that tree of life wait for me?

I got to work and my boss was there. Her name was Harmony. She was not only a boss, she was a great friend. My work consisted of scheduling events for mental-health consumers. I took people that were dealing with their own illnesses of the mind and eased their pain with involvement in the community. One activity goes a long way when you have someone who is trying to reason right within them. But sometimes no one showed up for the activities, and I wondered if they were not interested or maybe it was I who was turning them away with my thoughts. Happy Friday.

I left work and got back on the bus to go home, and immediately I thought I saw them. I'm sure: the eyes of Madonna. I sat next to her. Her curly black hair was irresistible and her posture was perfect. Should I say something? What should I do? Do anything? I remembered my promise.

I got home and had to cook supper early. Marlene, a staff member at the small options home where I lived, (a small group home for people living with mental illness) was there. She was a lady who cared so much. She made sure everything was good. Keith, one of my roommates, was going to see his mother that weekend. He loved buses. He could tell you about any bus, anywhere in Canada. He traveled across Canada twice a year. He would go to Vancouver, wait twenty minutes, and come home. He especially loved Greyhound.

Richard, my other roommate, went out in the morning and then came home; that was it. I think his reality had limited him to that.

After supper, I went to the YMCA to play basketball. I got back on another bus and sat in the middle. People started looking at me; they were disgusted at my thoughts. It felt like I was carrying shit in my gym bag. The only thing that could comfort me was basketball. Happy Friday.

I played ball for a good hour to an hour and a half. I had a good jumper, but passing was my best asset to the game. The same people showed up most of the time. I thought that they had gotten to know my thoughts like they did my free throws—consistent yet sometimes off. I never asked any of them if they could read my mind. If you wanted to find me anywhere on Friday nights, I was at the Y.

I took the bus home, and there they were: the eyes. If beauty is the word, she was beyond it. But I finally realized why I looked for Madonna's eyes when I should have been looking for the eyes of someone who understood me. Although both are very hard to find, I would rather have perfection forever than a moment of passion. The eyes of Madonna would be nice, but someone searching for the eyes of Adam would be better.

I would keep my promise. My promise to the father of us all, who is in us all, who loves us all.

I got home, and I heard Richard upstairs, laughing a good laugh. I did not know about fate or karma, whether I'd made this world of loneliness or was living what we could call the truth. All I knew was one thing: Almost every evening, I was alone, with Richard upstairs in his room. He was there, just because he was. I went to bed, read my Bible, and said my prayers, wondering what dreams would appear in my sleep. Thank you, Friday.

45. BACK

I couldn't walk down the street without my head being filled with voices. Either I was reading minds without trying to, hearing whispers from good spirits or bad, or realizing that my mind was filling everyone else's head. It hurt more than pain can describe, the dark blending with hope, the light trying to bring hope to itself. I saw people I used to have great conversations with, and I tried to say hello but they just walked by, trying not to look at me. If they did look at me, there was fire in their faces; they seemed to be angry about thoughts I couldn't control. It was a war that went on and on. Many more stays in the hospital were of no use; medication slowed the pace of war but did not bring composure.

I was in a daze. Doctors kept telling me that my reality was not real. I tried to reason within myself that it was an illness, that more treatment would bring comfort to jittery ideas and loose logic. But I couldn't shake the world within me, my turbulent life, my tangled environment. Time should have unraveled the lost sanity that was my experience, but this ordeal was hard to handle. Only one being could help ease the agony this world had become: Jesus. All of this took me back. I had to go back to the cabin where my celestial intervention had taken place. Maybe my world could change again.

46. WAIT

The sky is red, telling sailors about good mornings and good catches on the early rise. Everything is still, calm, collecting the senses of nature and blowing it into a breeze onto the ocean. The sea itself is tame, creamy on the shore.

The Whynots have just heard the story of Adam Jack Pelley, from basketball miracles to deals with entities beyond our perception. Promises now realized. His juice and pop almost gone, Adam stands up.

"Would you guys like to follow me?" he asks.

"Sure," Turner says. Sherri is a bit hesitant. Turner is awestruck by Adam, knowing that he feels a Band-Aid on your knee is the same as his medication, his Band-Aid on his brain. He thinks back to Mark and Susan, and what he now feels is their bleeding of spirit, medication the bandage. He realizes that every patient has a soul, a reality that is just as real as the love he feels for Sherri. Adam has his own reality, a schizophrenic stage; maybe that's why he is out here. Why he is out here is what Turner wants to understand.

With the daylong conversation, Turner realizes the potential Adam has, the potential that Adam once felt. Adam's story makes Turner realize that his father was right: all his patients have potential. But there is something about Adam, something more, something fresh, something worth understanding. With his wandering eye, Turner notices the pill bottles of clozapine and other prescription drugs sitting near the window sill.

Sherri is irritated. This is what all this waiting was for? A man living in a small cabin by himself?

Turner is convinced Adam's environment shapes his reality; it may be why every person with mental illness is the way he or she is. Turner's father made him come out here to meet Adam for a reason. Maybe Adam's reality is the one that is true. Turner's father wanted him to know that every person has a spirit; maybe Turner finding his own would make him a complete physician. Adam's story makes Turner realize he, Turner himself, has a soul, but Sherri isn't convinced.

They go out to the cliffs where the Whynots first encountered Adam. Adam sits down,

"Will you join me?"

Turner looks at his wife and sits down. Sherri stands there, her arms folded on her chest, thinking about her Christmas Day tragedy.

"I know you can't be a king, so who do you think you are?" she asks. "The beast or Jesus?" She doesn't know much about the Bible, but she knows the end, like most people. It is June 6, Adam's birthday. It is the sixth day, the sixth month. The number of the beast has three sixes; two is enough for her. But his name truly is Adam, the first. Could he be the last?

"Your asking me that question shows that you believe in God," Adam says. "That matters the most. As for your question, I don't know. How about you decide? If you are looking for answers, they have been here for two thousand years."

Sherri looks at Adam, and her whole life view changes in one second. She then realizes why Adam is out here. That these cliffs and the crashing sea are some of the few untouched loves of God's creation that are still apparent today. Adam has experienced that love before, and he still experiences that love now. The breaking of the tide, the smell of the trees, the view of a perfect picture that has yet to be painted—this is God's blank page. Turner has learned during the course of the day, listening to every word as his dad would have wanted. Sherri now believes that every word spoken today has meant something. She is here because there is love beyond what is seen or sensed.

"Sit, please," Adam says.

Sherri sits next to her husband. They look out at the ocean. That's all; they just look.

"Just as the sea is forgotten, because man believes he has discovered all of it, God has been forgotten, so we must discover him again. There is more to the sea than the surface."

The Whynots want to sit there all night with him, but they have to go.

"Can we come back so we can talk some more?" Turner asks.

"I'll be here, waiting."

The three stand, say their goodbyes, and the Whynots start on the path to their car before it gets too dark. They want to know what he is waiting for, but they never ask.

"Turner," Adam yells before he gets too far away.

"Yes,"

"The beginning and the end are the same, my friend." From knights learning about truth to pirates who only want the prize, to a tree of life and a promise that is kept through belief, only time will tell when things begin again. Turner looks at Adam and smiles, then waves goodbye.

Time passes quickly; they hurry carefully on the path so they can get to their car before night falls. Over the tree, along the edge. They get in the car and start to drive away from the day of the promise.

There is silence in the car until they are close to home, on Highway 103. Sherri asks, "So what are we going to do until we go see him again?"

"Do what we have always been doing," Turner answers. "Wait."